foundation course

graphic design

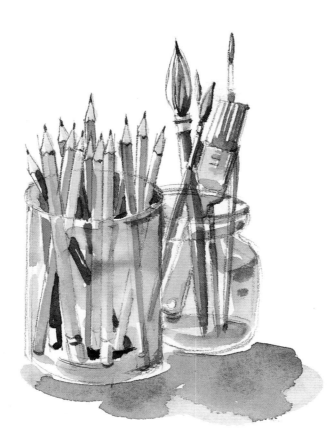

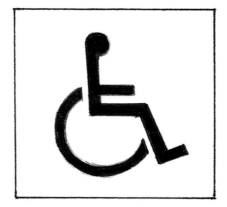  

foundation course

graphic design

Curtis Tappenden
Luke Jefford
Stella Farris

First published in Great Britain in 2004 by Cassell Illustrated
a division of Octopus Publishing Group Ltd.
2–4 Heron Quays, London E14 4JP

Text and design © 2004 Octopus Publishing Group Ltd.

Series development, editorial, design and layouts by
Essential Works Ltd.

Distributed in the United States of America by
Sterling Publishing Co., Inc.,
387 Park Avenue South, New York, NY 10016-8810

A CIP catalogue record for this book is available from
the British Library.

ISBN 1 84403 220 5
EAN 9781844032204

Printed in China

Contents

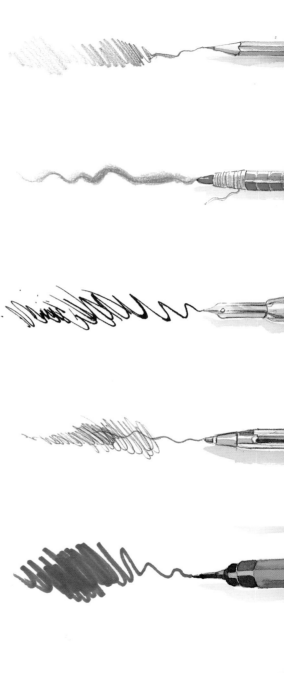

Introduction

Graphic design is by no means a new field. The terms used to describe the profession may have changed with the times – commercial art and visual communication being two previous titles – but the practice has remained centred on two main elements: images and words. Usually, they appear together and their combination can create a powerful and persuasive form of communication, whether in the context of advertising, packaging, books, magazines, television, or most recently, web design. This book is intended to lead you into the world of practical graphic design.

Design Basics considers the tools and materials you require and provides a clear technique-led guide to how best to use them. It includes exercises for expanding creative possibilities using thinking, sketching and clear methodical drawing to help you to carry ideas successfully through to completed graphic design projects. You will gain an appreciation of typefaces and an understanding of how to use them correctly. Appropriate application of letterforms to images is a key element of graphic design and in some cases can raise the profile of a commercial layout to the level of high art. The related crafts of photography, illustration and printmaking are also outlined in this book with live examples gleaned from the portfolios of design students and the professionals. Visualizing in three-dimensions has a key place in the world of graphic

design and you will also be introduced to the various facets of packaging and paper engineering, from 'pop-ups' to 'point of sale' materials.

The means of combining text and image using a desktop design package are now easily available, but clear guidance and practical advice can help you transform a satisfactory solution into one that exceeds levels of expectation. Computers and Production addresses many questions and concerns, where the science may have blinded your clear comprehension of computing and design and it goes a stage further in helping you to consider the necessary procedures for sending work to print.

With the basics in place you will be ready to enter the Masterclasses. This section examines a range of graphic design projects from the planning stage to completion. You will be shown the best approaches to various subjects and along with full step-by-step instructions, you will be given a professional's insight into the tips and tricks of the trade.

Foundation Course: Graphic Design offers a wide range of possibilities to both the eager beginner and fully-fledged professional, and has been carefully constructed to inspire and raise your levels of expectation and achievement. Whether you are a teacher or a student, in an educational environment or at home, this book is for you.

A history of graphic design

Beginnings

Words and pictures were first combined around four thousand years ago on Ancient Egyptian scrolls, and the medieval monks continued this tradition with their handwritten gospels exquisitely decorated with elaborate colour and gold leaf. A conscious decision to balance text against illustrations for the greatest visual impact can be seen in the work of French illustrator Geoffroy Tory (1480–1553). He also constructed letterforms drawn against the accurately scaled human figure and face. However, it was probably the advent of mechanical printing – pioneered by Johann Gutenberg when he started to print with metal blocks in the mid fifteenth century – that initiated the most radical changes. These changes and developments brought about distinct design and communications industries, and eventually led to the creation in the middle of the twentieth century of the discipline now known as graphic design.

The eighteenth and nineteenth centuries

Until the development of technologies to allow the use of colour for posters and periodicals, printed images and words were creatively composed in black and white as inked and non-inked space. The mechanical processes of 'intaglio' and 'gravure' printing (in which the plate was etched or incised below the surface) were applied creatively to meet a new demand for mass production.

The art of typography is rooted in the geometric elegance of the Roman alphabet, whose proportion and symmetry is still as

Johann Gutenberg, the pioneer of mechanical printing.

Troupe de
MLLE ÉGLANTINE

Eglantine
Jane Avril

Cléopatre
Gazelle

influential today as it was at the advent of mass produced publications. In the eighteenth century the Italian Giambattista Bodoni (1740–1813) introduced elegant, legible, Classical typefaces. The Industrial Revolution in the nineteenth century demanded greater variations of type style with the more robust appearance needed to suit the heavier printing methods and wider uses in advertising, breeding bold and black serif types.

The burgeoning of popular entertainment in Paris and other large European cities at the end of the nineteenth century gave a huge boost to the development of graphics, particularly in the work of popular artists such as Jules Cheret (1836–1932), Henri de Toulouse Lautrec (1864–1901) and Edouard Vuillard (1868–1940). The economy with which they married image to letterforms through the painterly technique of

The growth of popular entertainment towards the end of the nineteenth century moved the development of graphics forward with the marriage of image and letterforms as shown in this poster by Toulouse Lautrec promoting the Troupe de Mlle Églantine.

lithography made their images literally stand out from the crowd. Clearly inspired by the contemporary enthusiasm for Japanese prints, bold, flat colour, keyline drawing and hand-rendered display lettering characterized the work of a whole generation of graphic artists.

Important developments in graphic design also grew out of the great artistic and philosophical movements of the period. The Arts and Crafts protagonist William Morris (1834–96) insisted that beauty should be present in daily life. He reacted against mechanized mass production by setting up a design workshop in 1861 that specialized in bespoke designed products for everyday use – furniture, textiles and wallpapers. The books designed for the hugely influential Kelmscott Press he founded in 1880 made conscious use of white space and a range of different fonts to serve various functions on the composed page.

The sophistication of late-nineteenth-century French poster art caught the public imagination in America and collecting them caught on as a fashionable pastime. The work of Alphonse Mucha (1860–1939) and Eugene Grasset (1841–1917) were especially influential. In 1892 the literary and fashion magazine Harper's printed elegant posters to advertise and promote their Christmas edition. Many were swift to follow this example. Edward Penfield (1866–1925) and Louis Rhead (1857–1926) used posters for commercial advertising, and such bold expressions gave a significant boost to the evolution of graphic design.

Meanwhile, in the elite cafés of Vienna as the nineteenth century was drawing to its close, artists and architects met to discuss the fresh ideas aired in the exciting new publication Studio. Also of interest were the latest exhibition catalogues, including those of the Secessionist group, which included the artists Gustav Klimt (1862–1918) and Egon Schiele (1890–1918), and others – who were developing a graphic language, rich in expression, with a synthesized fusion of illustration and text.

The early twentieth century

The early twentieth century saw exciting changes in the design world. The rebuilding of Europe after the First World War seemed to spur the creativity of design thinkers, and a number of idealistic design manifestos were the result. These created blueprints for modern living, free from the chaos left in the wake of war. For the privileged few, these ideals evolved into the decadence of Art Deco – a sharper, more optimistic philosophy revisiting the stylistic interpretations of Art Nouveau, but blending them with the simple iconographic symbols of ancient civilizations. In the 1920s counter movements such as Dadaism and Expressionism set themselves against the hard-edged, propagandist language of Constructivism – a movement of firmly structured rules – as its name suggests. Anti-establishment, anti-war and anti-design, Kurt Schwitters (1887–1948), George Grosz (1893–1959) and John Heartfield (1891–1968) created collaged layers of type and image, specifically chosen and structured to define the verbal content. It was the first time the studio artist/designer had full control over the layout, thereby by-passing the role of printer as decision-maker in the creative process. The importance of this move cannot be underestimated. A freer approach to the drawn image rapidly replaced the engraver's block, and there was a significant shift from hand-crafted methods to those of mass-production. Grasping the emerging opportunity, Walter Gropius (1883–1969), an architect and designer, founded the Bauhaus, an idealistic school of design, strongly influenced by the approach of William Morris. The principles of utility and artistic merit that guided the Bauhaus are considered fundamental in the later development of industrial and commercial design.

Commercial branding and trademarks also came into their own during the early twentieth century. In 1907 Peter Behrens (1868–1940) was appointed designer to the electrical company, Allgemeine Elektrizitäts Gersellschaft (AEG). He created a corporate 'house style' – a set of design rules that were applied consistently through all elements of the organization. His typeface Behrens-schrift created a solid and simplified brand image – it is still used with little adaptation to this day.

During this period, the demands of industry led to huge developments in graphic design. Influential designers led the way in typeface invention. Eric Gill (1882–1940), the British engraver and sculptor, created the Gill Sans and Perpetua type families. A Swiss typographer Adrian Frutiger (born 1928) designed Univers and its cousin Frutiger for Air France and the signage of Charles De Gaulle airport in Paris. The British typographer Stanley Morison (1889–1967) created the classic book font Times New Roman, one of the most widely used typefaces of all time. Typographic innovation continues today as new typefaces are developed to satisfy the ever-changing needs of contemporary design.

The post-war period

Following the Second World War the growth of consumerism opened the gate to a new generation of graphic styles. Examples include the aesthetically clean Milanese modernism first associated with Olivetti, Paul Rand's (1914–96) inimitable branding for IBM computers in the USA, and Saul Bass's (1920–96), sharp graphic title sequences and film posters for such classics as Otto Preminger's 1955 classic film The Man With The Golden Arm.

During the Cold War years American graphics vividly expressed the vitality and spirit of the West, notably through the United States Information Agency Magazine Amerika. The work of the eminent American typographer Herb Lubalin (1919–81) exemplified and developed these trends, and his contribution to the styling of magazines in the 1960s was considerable. The other great exponent of American graphic design from the 1960s, through record covers, magazines, posters and packaging, was Milton Glaser (b. 1929).

The Bauhaus building designed in 1925 by the arhitectural office of Walter Gropius.

The sixties and seventies

In the 1960s, advances in colour printing technology allowed strong pictorial symbols and bold display typefaces to be used ever more imaginatively. Influenced by the 'Pop' and 'Op' Art movements of the decade, packaging and corporate design, particularly in the fields of fashion and retailing, underwent a revolution. The design of LP record sleeves provided a hugely important showcase for innovative graphic design. Moving graphics were also explored through the expanding world of television.

The 1970s can be seen as the era of design consultancies, whose chief concern was to establish corporate identity programmes. Image-conscious businesses were keenly aware of the need to be seen and remembered in a highly competitive market. It was no longer a case of words and images communicating meaning but of instant recognition. Context would give meaning to graphic images emblazoned, for example, on the tail fins of the aircraft of major world airlines. The identities of Alitalia, British Airways, Japan Airlines and Singapore Airlines were designed by the same San Francisco agency, Landor Associates.

But just as corporate design as conceived by the major design consultancies was gaining ascendancy, a reaction to its dominant blandness was emerging in the form of the punk street style of the mid 1970s. Punk, with its desire to shock, infiltrated popular music, clothing and the independent style publications known as fanzines. Torn letters, handwriting and recycled images were deliberately photocopied or screen-printed by the young, raw designers Barney Bubbles (1942–83) and Jamie Reid (b. 1940), to produce crude anti-design. The punk process was highly significant for the future of graphic design. The designer gained direct control over the work at pre-press stage, often shooting the final artwork – type with image together – using a printer's process camera.

The eighties and nineties

The launch of Apple Macintosh computer in January 1984 was probably the most important event of the decade for graphic design. Typesetting was rendered obsolete and for the first time, designers could, in theory, create layouts on screen with no further need for process technicians. Shaping layouts before the eyes and changing their composition and colour at the press of a button was a dream come true. The use of computers brought a level of accuracy to the process never before seen. The placing of elements into a layout was no longer a matter of judgement by eye, and computer manipulation of images allowed changes to be effected rapidly to suit the tightest deadlines.

Stylistically, with the taming of punk came a cultural shift into Post-modernism and the eclectic gathering of graphic elements from various styles and genres. Young exponents, such as the British designer Neville Brody (b. 1957), re-worked magazine style in an exciting, hands-on way, stretching and redesigning display fonts to suit his needs and challenging the conventional grid templates set up in computer layout programs. Brody mixed and matched his letterforms on grids that broke all the rules, and yet still worked in visual terms. The Californian ex-surfer David Carson (b. 1956), took it all a stage further into a style known as 'deconstruction', where a deliberate disregard for the hierarchies of layout and typography created fragmentary displays of barely legible type, not dissimilar in visual terms to rhythmic, abstract paintings. The stimulating 'edge' carried by the music journal *Raygun*, was to redefine graphic design for a new generation of young designers.

The new millennium

The growing ease of access to increasingly sophisticated computer design technology has resulted in the crossing of borders between

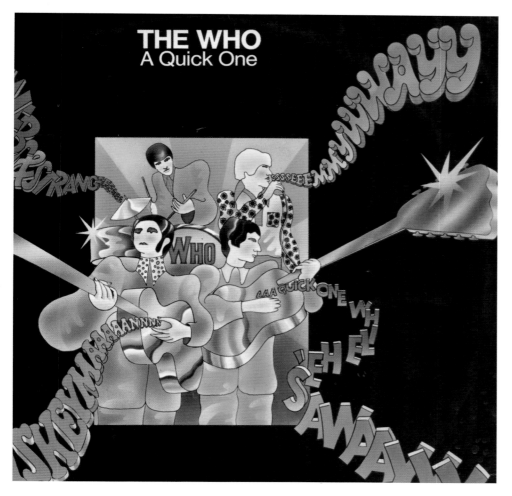

The design of LP sleeves has always provided a hugely important showcase for innovative graphic design. The Who's A Quick One *album sleeve from 1966 used LSD-inspired graphics.*

designers now work as freelancers, or in partnerships, for limited contracts. Indeed, diversity means the boundaries are always changing, and a conceptual fine artist who uses film or photography to interact with the audience is not so far away from the concept graphic designer who uses creative thinking for an interactive presentation or museum exhibition.

It is possible that this new century will see the term 'graphic designer' disappearing from use. Constant change is here to stay: work patterns have altered dramatically, and it has become harder to predict the impact of such changes on the societies that designers wish to influence. The driving force of consumerism will undoubtedly have a huge effect on the further development of the industry and how it presents itself. The prediction that printed matter would be totally replaced by electronic media has not come to pass. A computer is not like a newspaper. It is neither a cheap, nor readily disposable object that can be conveniently read and then thrown away; it serves a necessary but different function. What can be predicted is that as long as humans need to communicate visual information there will be a role for designers to facilitate and support such communication through whatever media are available.

graphic design and other creative professions. Film-making, self-publishing, music and multi-media presentation and website building have tended to become merged in a visual communications melting pot. The blurring of all previous distinctions means the design professional can become a jack of all trades as well as a master of one. The Internet has allowed the small players to compete with big corporations in the same markets for the same design contracts. Smaller co-operatives have emerged as a flexible alternative to the larger companies and many graphic

DESIGN BASICS

Pencils and pens

Formalizing your ideas into graphic images does not require sophisticated equipment. At the beginning of the design process, all you really need is a mark-making implement and a surface to draw on. A great deal can be learned from experimenting with a limited range of tools and materials. Using a pencil or pen will force you to focus on the types of mark that this simple tool can make.

Pencils

Lead or graphite pencils [*1*] *are available in twenty grades of two ranges: H and B. In the H range, 10H is the hardest. In the B range 10B is the softest.*

Mechanical or clutch pencils [*2*] *contain fine leads of 1 millimetre diameter or less. The size of the lead is usually marked on the spring-released shaft. Replacement leads are available.*

Coloured pencils [*3*] *are available in up to 72 colours. These provide a dry, controllable medium that is perfect for visualizing first ideas and for final artwork. Water-soluble pencils soften and break down into fluid runs of colour when water is added.*

Chinagraph pencils [*4*] *are soft, waxy pencils ideal for marking shiny surfaces, such as overlays or glass.*

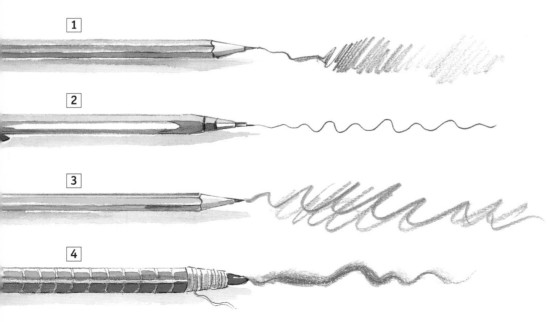

Pens

Dip or nib pens [*5*] *are sturdy and pressure sensitive and they produce a characterful, scratchy line. Nibs of various shapes and sizes can be obtained from an art supplier. They can be used with different inks. Indian ink is shellac-based, dense, waterproof black ink. Coloured inks are similar to Indian but have greater flow and translucency. They are not lightfast.*

Fountain pens [*6*] *are bladder- or reservoir-fed nib pens intended for writing but are equally suitable for drawing. Fountain pen ink is available in a number of colours.*

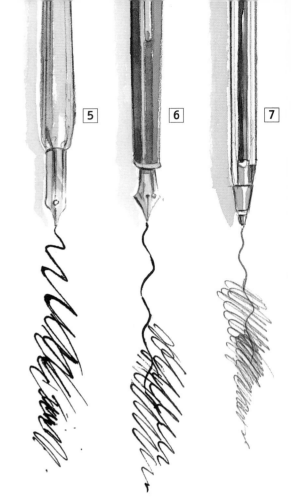

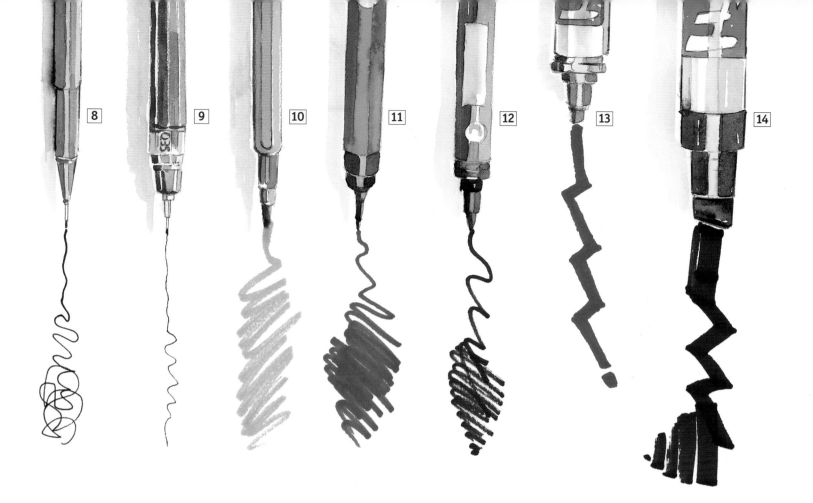

Ballpoint pens [7] deliver mechanical marks at an even, constant flow in a thick, dry, permanent ink. Cheap disposables are ubiquitous, but more expensive models that utilize refills are also available.

Fineliner and rolling ball pens [8] produce a more consistent width of line. They are available in many variations of nib and tip, and can be purchased filled with waterproof and non-waterproof inks. With so many sizes and shapes available, you need to try them out to see what works best for you.

Stylo-tipped pens [9] were developed for technical drawing where a sharp line is essential. A special tubular nib was developed to assist flow. There is a wide range of nib widths available and the size is always indicated on the side, often with a colour code. Two main types are rapidograph and isograph.

Felt-tip pens [10–12] have soft felt nibs that disperse concentrated ink. They are used where stronger, thicker lines are required and can be used effectively with ink marker pens.

Markers [13, 14] are round or chisel-tipped felt pens that can rapidly cover a surface with strong, water or spirit-based colour. On a layout pad the ink bleeds across the surface, and the spirit-based colours can be blended using petroleum distillates or white spirit.

Papers

Your choice of paper will depend on what drawing medium you have selected. Heavy, stretched paper or board with an absorbent, sized surface is best for wet media. Coated, slightly shiny papers and boards are excellent for fine pen work. Various qualities of cartridge paper are suitable for general pencil/pen work. Some artists' papers are sold in imperial sizes (measured in inches), while designer papers are usually available in A sizes (measured in millimetres). These sizes are standard for all stationery, printers and photocopiers.

A Size chart

A0   841 x 1188mm/33.1 x 46.8 in
A1   594 x 841mm/23.4 x 33.1 in
A2   420 x 594mm/16.5 x 23.4 in
A3   297 x 420mm/11.7 x 16.5 in
A4   210 x 297mm/8.3 x 11.7 in
A5   148 x 210mm/5.8 x 8.3 in
A6   105 x 148mm/4.1 x 5.8 in

Paper types

Cartridge paper [1] is a generally inexpensive, machine-made, general-purpose paper available in various colours, sizes and qualities and can be bought in pads, books or individual sheets. It should be stretched for wet media.

Watercolour papers [2] are 'hot-pressed' (HP), 'cold-pressed' (CP or NOT), and 'rough', and contain a textured grain suitable for loose, wet pigment. Hot-pressed is smooth and excellent for gouache or flat washes, cold-pressed is a good all-rounder, and rough is ideal for producing textures. Available as ply board or in sheets. The ply board can be 'stripped' off so that the thin top layer holding the image can be stored or scanned.

Bristol board, CS10 and Ticket card [3] are smooth, heavy cards. They are best suited to fine pen work, marker pens and inks. Other coated papers and cards are usually used for leaflets or packaging where a shiny look is required. Experiment with samples to find out what suits your needs.

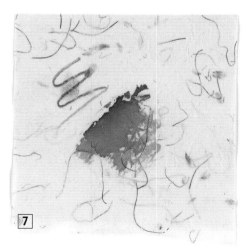

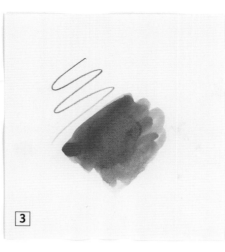

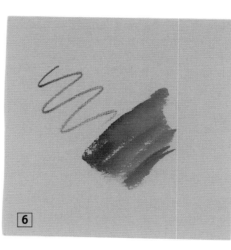

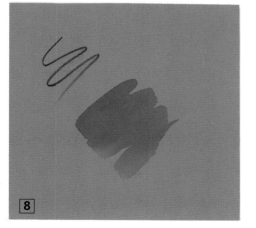

Tracing paper [4] is a thin, translucent paper that allows you to see an image beneath so that you can copy it. Available in sheets and pads. Layout paper is thin and white. It has the quality of cartridge paper but is translucent like tracing paper, making it perfect for visualizing and copying.

Detail paper [5] is a heavy-duty layout paper suitable for marker pens.

Pastel paper [6] is a grainy paper type, ideal for creating visual images requiring a slight, textured surface. These papers are available in a many colours.

Hand-made papers [7] are attractive, textured papers ideal for backgrounds and collaged layers.

Coloured papers [8] are ideal for collage work where blocks of colour are required. There is a wide range of colours and some are available in self-adhesive forms.

Acetate [9] is a thin transparent plastic that can be used in photocopiers and printers. It can be used as an overlay, and used to position type over artwork. Permanent, spirit-based inks adhere to its shiny surface as do acrylic paints.

Paints and brushes

Choice of paint is important to the final intention of the work you are undertaking, and roughs and visuals require a different level of rendering to a final piece of artwork. Brushes also need careful consideration, and the most proficient, hand-rendered graphic artworks are those that combine a variety of strokes made by different mark-makers.

Paints

The graphic designer may use paints to create roughs and visuals. It is also important for a designer/art director to have an understanding of media and of different styles and techniques in order to commission artworks effectively.

Watercolours [1] *are sold in either tubes or solid blocks. Tubes can be wasteful and when hardened, they are much more difficult to soften and re-use. A set of twelve colours is adequate for a basic design kit.*

Gouache [2], *also known as designer colour or poster colour, are the paints most commonly used by graphic designers. Usually bought in tubes, they are basically an opaque form of watercolour with added chinese white or chalk, which causes the colours to lay with a dense, matt flatness. As well as being laid as solid colour, gouache can be diluted and applied with the fluidity of watercolour.*

Acrylic [3] *is a highly versatile medium that adheres to most surfaces. Acrylic can be used effectively with thick brushwork or soft washes. Acrylics are available in tubes, jars, squeezy bottles, and in liquid form in bottles.*

Brushes

Brushes are produced in two main shapes: flat and round. The most expensive brush material is the reddish Kolinsky sable (a Siberian relative of the mink) and the cheapest is a synthetic fibre mix. It is a good idea to purchase the best you can afford, as a good quality brush that is well cared for should last for many years. When selecting round brushes check that the hairs can be brought easily to a fine point and that the head is springy enough to hold plenty of paint. Round brushes range from size 0000 to 26. They are the most common brush shape used by the designer, because they offer both broad strokes and finer, delicate strokes. Flat brushes are square-ended, come in various sizes and deliver broad washes or smaller, chisel-shaped strokes.

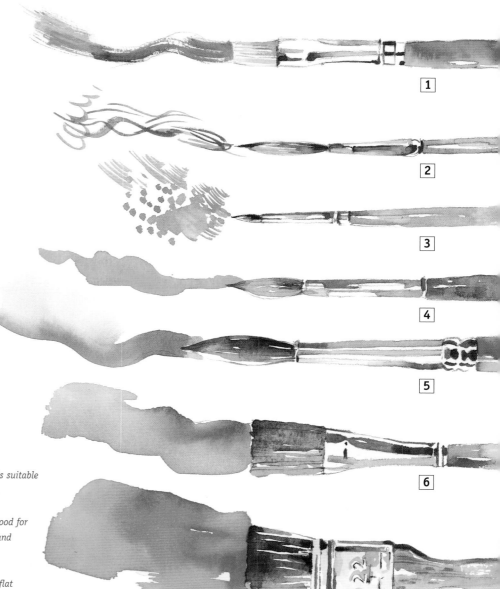

A **hog hair flat brush** [1] has stiff hairs that are useful for a thicker paint medium such as acrylic.

A **rigger** [2], as its name suggests, was used for painting the ornamentation on ships. With long, springy hair, it can be guided beautifully around curves and is a favourite of signwriters and calligraphers.

A **spotter** [3] is the shortest of the round brushes. It has a very fine point and is especially useful for those who work in miniature.

A **medium round brush** [4] is suitable for delicate watercolour work.

A **large round brush** [5] is good for broad strokes of watercolour and moderately fine detail.

A **wash brush** [6] is set in a flat ferrule (the metal cap that holds the hairs in place) with a wide, wooden handle. It is best used for large washes.

A **flat brush** [7] is similar to a wash brush but has longer, stiffer hairs. They are best suited to the one-stroke line, or for blending tones.

TIP:

Never leave brushes standing in a pot of water because they will lose their shape. Clean the hairs thoroughly, right down to the *ferrule*, with warm soapy water and soften the hairs back into a point using spittle or soap.

Useful tools

When looking at professional examples of graphic design, it may be hard to envisage the process that led to the glossy, final product. Most final artwork is now computer generated but many design studios still follow a more traditional design process, beginning with thumbnail sketches. These early sketches are often produced with traditional drawing tools, which should be to hand in every design studio.

In order to meet a tight deadline, it can still be quicker at the start of the design process to cut and paste type and images by hand. First ideas still tend to be scribbled onto a pad, an item that should always be close to hand. In the initial excitement generated by the advent of desktop publishing it was thought that all non-digital processes would be shelved. However, it seems that many designers need the space to work manually – to gather their thoughts or mull over ideas – and this is often easier away from the intensity of the computer screen. Also, in cases where a project involves illustrative or textured material, parts of the whole need to be created by hand before they can be scanned in.

In addition to the items described here, you may also find it useful to have a drawing board, an angle-poise lamp and a lightbox for viewing transparencies.

Spring bow compasses

Ruler

Flexible curve

Drawing and measuring

The essential drawing aid is a good ruler. In addition, you may need the following:
• A pair of spring bow compasses, small radius compasses, and a ruling pen are very useful for basic technical drawing. Ruling pens have two adjustable prongs through which ink runs. The wider they are opened, the thicker the line. They can be dipped into ink or paint, and do not clog easily.
• A flexible curve is a flexible metal rod encased in a square rubber conduit. It can be shaped smoothly into a perfect curve to suit your purpose.
• Set squares are triangular plastic instruments manufactured in various sizes to facilitate the accurate drawing of lines of different angles. An adjustable version enables most angles to be set.

Adjustable set square

Dry-mount aerosol adhesive

Rubber gum

PVA glue

Gluestick

Masking tape

Gum strip

Pencil sharpeners are a vital accessory for accurate drawing.

Gluing and mounting

There are a number of adhesives that are specially formulated for design work.

• Petroleum-based rubber gum (cow gum) is useful where clean gluing is essential. Applied with a spatula, excess gum can be rubbed off the paper with fingers when dry, leaving no residue.

• PVA (polyvinyl-acetate) glue is a white plastic emulsion-based adhesive. Once dry, it is transparent. It is a multi-purpose adhesive appropriate for wood, plastic, paper and card/cardboard.

• Gluesticks are useful for small pieces of work, but not so good for repositioning.

• Dry-mount aerosol spray adhesive is popular in the area of display graphics, but it dries out over time and the glued work may peel off. It is also hazardous if inhaled. Use it only in a well-ventilated room away from the main work area.

• Masking tape is most commonly used for masking edges of artwork. It is useful for temporarily mounting or positioning.

• Gum strip (brown paper tape) adheres to wood or paper when dampened. It is mainly used for taping sheets of stretched paper into position.

Cutting

You will need a selection of sharp cutting tools.

• Craft knives have interchangeable blades for cutting heavy-duty card and other materials.

• A scalpel is a surgical instrument for fine, craft cutting, and most effective in cutting and pasting. Blades can be changed to suit specialist tasks.

• Scissors are an essential item and investing in a good quality pair is worthwhile.

Craft knife

Scalpel

Scissors

Workspace and materials

Keeping an ordered, well-maintained workspace is particularly important for a graphic designer. Whether you work in a corner of your living room or a large studio, you need to function with ease, having materials and equipment to hand, and plenty of places where work can be stored flat and kept clean and dry. Sound work habits are worth adopting because they are undoubtedly reflected in the work you produce for your clients.

You should work at a robust desk – one that is large and strong enough to hold your computer equipment. Other items, such as a drawing board, desktop scanner or printer can be placed on a separate surface.
• Lamps should be placed to provide good lighting for your work surface and so that no shadow is cast onto your work.
• Keep pencils and felt tip pens either in their box or in a pot so that the correct colour can be easily selected. Stand brushes in a jar or pot, bristles upwards.
• Guard against your inks and paints drying out by always replacing the lids and caps after use. It will also reduce the risk of spillage.
• A small chest of drawers or filing cabinet provides good storage for your materials, or if you prefer they can be stored on shelves for easier access.
• A plan chest with large, shallow drawers is ideal for storing paper flat. Large portfolio carrying cases are a cheaper, temporary alternative. Work should be kept clean in transparent, plastic sleeves that clip into the plastic coated, zip-up covers. Portfolios can be bought in all A sizes.

The graphic designer who needs to transport tools and equipment to work or college, should consider investing in a fishing tackle box, which provides ideal portable storage. Produced in a range of sizes, they are relatively inexpensive and are available from angling shops and some sports and recreation stores. There are handy compartments for erasers and other small items, hinged trays for drawing implements, long slots for rules and brushes and a deep well for larger pieces of equipment such as paint tubes or ink bottles.

TIP:

It is a good idea to avoid having to constantly reach across your worktop, so if you are right-handed, consider having the items you use most to your right or vice versa if you are left-handed.

Small markers

Rulers kept in long tray in top shelf

Felt-tip pens kept together with elastic bands

Drawing instruments, such as set squares, kept in tray

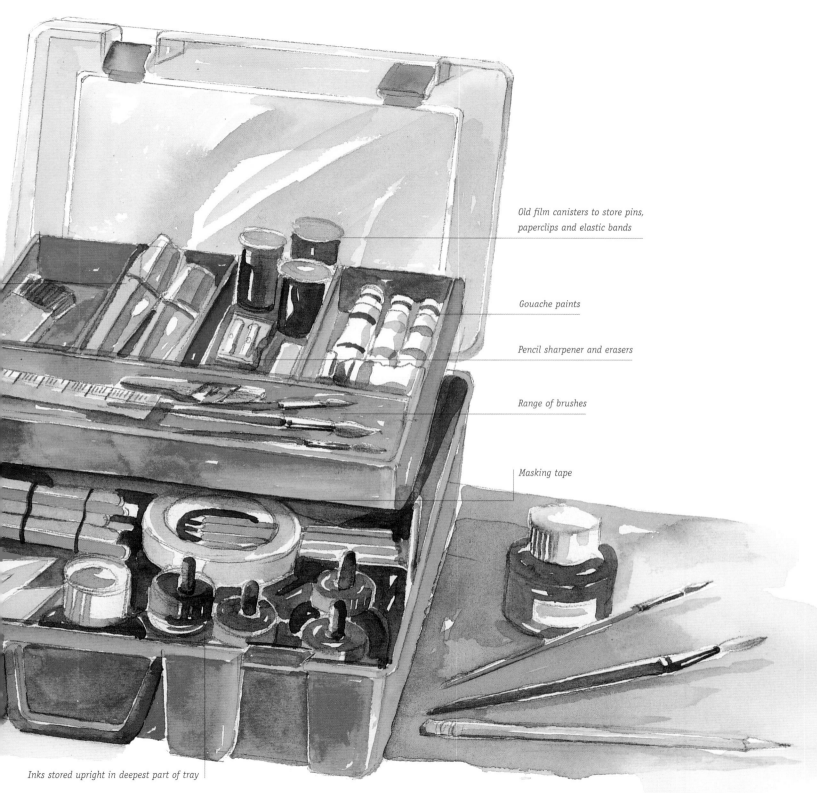

Old film canisters to store pins,
paperclips and elastic bands

Gouache paints

Pencil sharpener and erasers

Range of brushes

Masking tape

Inks stored upright in deepest part of tray

Making marks and sketching

Graphic designers need to communicate a subject or idea quickly, clearly and simply. So it is good to learn to develop your mark-making in an uncomplicated but effective way. There is no right or wrong way to draw and a variety of media can be used to visualize a design. Provided that your sketches make sense of the developing idea, then they are correct.

A designer needs to be able to gather reference material quickly, and organize and present it with clear drawing skills. This is a working process that takes the seeds of an idea and visualizes them effectively, facilitating the production – hand-drawn or computerized – of the final product.

Sources

Developing any idea into a graphic product such as a logo, advertisement or piece of packaging requires original source material. This is best from primary sources – your own photograph, digital image, or illustrative sketch. Good secondary sources include magazines, books, the Internet, leaflets, cuttings, or found objects and materials.

These you can trace, sketch, photocopy, cut, paste and recompose as you work. You should be careful how you use your reference material so you do not infringe copyright through plagiarism (presenting someone else's work as your own). Always significantly change the work to make it your own, and where the design needs to directly relate in style or content to another creator, then it is important that you make that clear to your client.

Effective mark-making

Pencil marks are controllable and can create lines with an enormous range of qualities and textures. A strong visual will display what are known as 'weightings' of line. Application of pressure on the

Scribbling is useful for urgent first jottings, and quickly capturing thoughts and ideas.

Cross-hatching is repeated parallel lines, criss-crossing at angles to each other. It can be used to create shading and texture, and areas of light and dark.

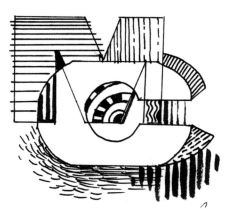

You can display the **illusion of tone or depth** with line alone, by altering the spaces between drawn parallel lines.

pencil reinforces a line, communicating a stronger physical structure. Where a drawing is in perspective, the points furthest away may be drawn with a lighter stroke to help to achieve the illusion of depth. Full line weighting delivered by a thicker, heavily pressured stroke actually highlights the form of the subject drawn (especially where it is three-dimensional), and 'lifts' it away from other elements. Although pencil is wonderfully expressive, many graphic designers prefer pen marks for initial sketches and more technical finishes. The pen can render exciting variations of tonal and linear mark-making. A flexible nib allows you to bring the line to life – a rich variety of marks can be achieved by altering the pressure that is applied.

Practise these techniques and, try to apply them to the ideas you are developing. These are starting points, and it is possible that the marks themselves may prompt further thoughts and development of ideas. Their application will certainly enhance your visuals and ideas sheets.

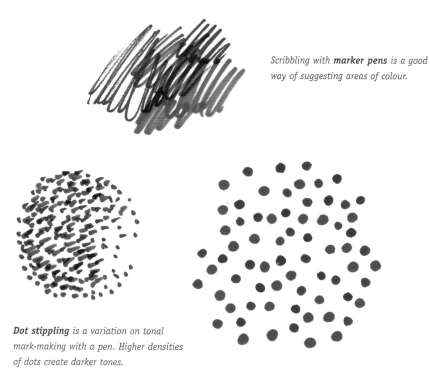

*Scribbling with **marker pens** is a good way of suggesting areas of colour.*

Dot stippling is a variation on tonal mark-making with a pen. Higher densities of dots create darker tones.

Colour and texture

Your choice of colour medium for your visuals can contribute to the overall character of the design you are trying to convey, whether precise and graphic or free and painterly. Experiment with different paints and inks to learn about the special qualities of each medium.

Pastel is pigment in stick form. There are two types: oil and chalk. Although pastels are messier than pen or pencil, they can be used to create vibrant colour – a cross between drawing and painting. Pastel drawings need to be 'fixed' with an aerosol spray fixative to prevent smudging.

Acrylic is useful because it can be used on surfaces other than paper. It is possible to paint your visualizations onto glass or plastic working models with this medium.

Gouache has a matt opacity that means that it can produce a flat finish. However, this takes practice to achieve. It is a useful medium for both draft sketches and final artwork.

Ink can be used to create more intense washes than are possible with watercolours.

Watercolour, in design work, is principally a tinting medium, excellent for rendering in three-dimensions. Keep washes fluid with crisp edges and do not worry about watermarks or ridges that appear between washes. These give your working drawings a lively, fresh feel.

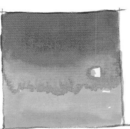

Marker blends are tricky to use and practise is required to perfect the technique. Blending with markers is a slick alternative to a watercolour wash. Smooth blends can be achieved with similar hues of marker getting progressively lighter or darker. Spirit markers can also be blended with white spirit or petroleum distillates, and gently merged into the image with a soft cloth or cotton wool.

Creative thinking

Creative visual thinking is a process that is usually best approached as a problem-solving discipline. In other words to achieve a feasible solution, creative thinking and practical problem-solving need to happen at the same time. In order to formulate your ideas and communicate them clearly, you need to take a systematic approach. It is helpful to break the process down into five stages.

Types of creative thinking

Groups of ideas – 'concepts' – are the creative solutions to design problems. Concepts and ideas cannot be forced: and solutions can often be stumbled upon by accident. Ideas may occur unexpectedly in the middle of the night or under the pressure of a morning shower. However, once a basic concept is in place, there should be sound reasons for your choice of imagery, colour, typography and composition. From this point, the elements chosen must reflect the objectives of the brief and communicate their message clearly. There are a number of helpful methods for stimulating creative thinking that will help you formulate your ideas clearly and enable you to present them visually.

Free thinking

This is also known as brainstorming, and it involves making a list of anything, however tenuous or silly it might seem, that comes to mind concerning a subject. The main thing is not to worry about what anyone might think of your ideas, and to open your mind and think as freely as possible.

Structured thinking

You may find it helpful to create a flow chart or diagram to help structure your thinking. Each stage should be represented by a key word or symbol representing the action to be taken. The sequence should be linked by lines and arrows in the direction of flow. Keep flow charts simple so that the process and aims are completely clear.

Visual thinking

Simple signs and symbols can convey powerful positive or negative meanings. They can be used to stir emotion, warn, grab attention, puzzle and provoke. Danger signs such as the skull and crossbones is a good example. Sketching and doodling will help you create your own symbols and explore different ways to transmit your message clearly.

Lateral thinking

Unlike logical, or linear, thinking, lateral, or sideways, thinking can help us see a problem from a new perspective in order to find original solutions. If we break away from logic and think laterally, we can come up with creative and surprising insights that can upturn preconceptions and lead to eye-catching designs.

EXERCISE

Consider part of an ordinary day, perhaps from the time you woke up to the time you arrived at work. Think about key events: focus on the things you saw or thought, your journey to work, people you met, and then write them down. Select no more than ten events that you feel are significant and are easy to represent visually. Create a flow diagram of your day reducing the information to simple signs and symbols. Compose it with a variation of colour, mark, scale and texture. However, the level of finish is not the most important consideration, the focus is creative thinking and conveying information clearly. Use combinations of tools and techniques.

Composition

The arrangement of the different elements in a design is known as composition. A design may work well because the images and type complement each other in colour, scale, texture and so on. Or, they may contrast violently, creating a more violent impact. It is often good to follow your instincts where design is concerned, but there are a few basic design principles that should be explored and understood, before you can break the rules.

Principles of composition

Good composition is shapes, forms and colours all working together in a unified, dynamic whole. Most graphic design layouts are made up of elements such as images, headings or titles and blocks of main text. If you squint at the design, the different elements appear as blocks of colour and tone. With this in mind, the composition game can be played simply using blocks that represent these core elements. They can be moved around, enlarged or reduced, and cropped to explore a range of design alternatives.

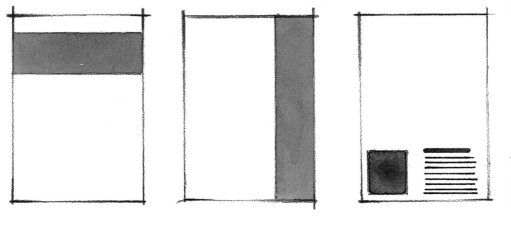

Thirds. Compositions appear balanced when the primary focus occupies a third of the design grid. The remaining two thirds assume a secondary role, attracting less attention. One third could be 'empty' to balance the other two type- or image-filled thirds.

Symmetry. Shapes that mirror one another on the paper are symmetrical. Although symmetry is often a classic, pleasing effect, it does not always provoke the most lively response. Neither does the main element have to be set in the very centre in order to be the focus of the design. Asymmetric compositions are often more effective because the eye is stimulated and attracted by contrasts and dynamic mismatching.

Space. *It is often not what is put into a composition that is most important, but what is left out. Empty space around a stronger or busier element such as an image or text can draw attention to it. Equally, a composition that has little empty space, but is well conceived with layered or interlocking elements can also work well, particularly where the layers all hold different textures.*

Rhythm. *The way in which elements are combined in a composition can give it a sense of movement or balance. Repetition of mark, pattern and colour can work together in much the same way as the tempo in music – the rhythm can be regular or irregular, and this rhythm can be used to guide the eye.*

EXERCISE

Look at symmetry, space and rhythm, and make small thumbnail sketches to illustrate different examples of the points made here. Do not use type or images. Merely substitute shapes and bands in a range of tones and fit them creatively into simple rectangular grids. When you have practised drawing multiple variations of composition, select examples from the working world and consider how well they are composed. Use tracing paper to copy the different elements of an advertisement or poster, then cut out the shapes and combine them in a different order.

Simulating 3-D

Designers often need to communicate three-dimensional shapes, and where an object has a specific function, it often needs detailed planning through isometric drawings and perspective diagrams. At its most basic level, 3-D (three-dimensional) drawing simulates the effect of depth and gives shapes form and volume. The ability to simulate a 3-D surface using light and shade is essential to every designer.

EXERCISE

Create five basic shapes using five different media – pencil, pen, watercolour, gouache and cut paper. Apply tonal values to these shapes to give them a 3-D form. Use each medium differently to achieve a three-dimensional effect. Simple exercises like these are invaluable for gaining confidence and technical proficiency with a variety of media.

Light and dark

The simplest shaded pencil scribble can indicate how light is falling and simulate volume. Where your three-dimensional rendering is not copied through direct observation, you will need to impose an imaginary light source. Areas of an object that face the light are nearest the light source and will be paler, and those furthest away will be darker. Areas of shadow will reinforce the illusion of a three-dimensional shape.

Pencil shading for design visuals need not be painstakingly undertaken. Brisk, directional lines are more than adequate to communicate a rough shape. Where a tonal scale is added, the rough shape is transformed into a cylinder.

Pen strokes in a criss-cross pattern (cross-hatching) can be used to build up a web of tone that adds volume to the basic cone shape. Areas of cross-hatching can be added to create depth with light and shade.

  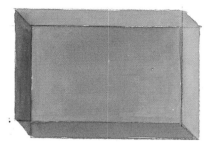

Watercolour is fluid, translucent and rapid, and excellent for small, colourful visuals. Dark and light areas can create the illusion of depth. Layers of paint can be applied one on top of the other to produce darker tones. The lighter tones can be achieved by diluting the paint with water.

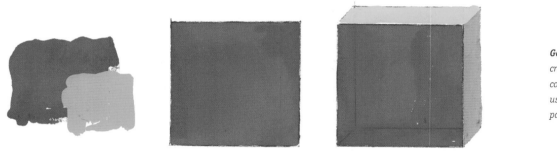

Gouache mixed to the consistency of single cream can be applied to create solid blocks of colour. Add white to lighten the tone. When using gouache always take care to mix the paints thoroughly to avoid streaks.

Textured papers and flat-coloured papers can be cut sharply or with rough edges, depending on the desired effect. Move the cut shapes around to find the most effective arrangement before finally sticking the pieces down. A thin sliver of light cream card was added to the top of the circle to transform it into a sphere.

Introducing colour

With its power to control and dictate responses, colour is one of the chief tools of the graphic designer. Learning and understanding how it can be used to influence choices, sell products, and generally enhance designs is a major part of training. By using aptly selected combinations of colour, you can be confident that your message can be communicated to best effect.

The naming of colour

Colour is described according to various characteristics and properties. Hue is the characteristic that distinguishes one colour from another, that is, what makes it blue rather than red. The hue is the term marked on a tube paint or process colour (colour for print). Chroma, or saturation, refers to the intensity of a colour. The primary colours – red, yellow and blue – have the highest levels of saturation. Diluting colour pigments with either water or spirit weakens their intensity. Adding white to the hue also reduces its colour saturation, creating a tint, whereas adding black or a dark colour creates a shade. A colour can be neutralized by mixing it with its complement (see the colour wheel, below).

The colour wheel

Each hue contrasts most strongly with its opposite, or complementary colour on the wheel (see illustration, left) green is complementary to red, orange to blue, and violet to yellow. The most harmonious combinations sit next to each other on the wheel – for example, yellow and orange or green and blue. It is theoretically possible to mix any colour from permutations of the primaries, red, yellow and blue.

Colour temperature

Colours can be said to have 'warmth' or 'coolness'. Red, orange and yellow are warm and visually tend to jump forward into prominence in a piece of design. The cooler hues – blue, lilac and green – tend to recede in a design. Sensitivity to the use of colour in design is vital to enable you to make use of the differing emotional responses each colour evokes. Using colours judiciously can add poetry to the graphic designer's language. Strong hues shout loudly. Red is passionate and hot, the colour of fire and anger. In combination with black and white it stamps power and authority onto an image or branded product. Green, its complement, is naturally calming. It carries an association of freshness and life; the trees are clothed in leaves of green, and images of grassy meadows induce inner calm. Blue has a neutrality, which in its darker, brooding hues can border on the melancholy, whereas its brighter tints and shades convey a joyous optimism.

Colour in graphic design

Colour must serve four main functions: to attract attention; to hold attention; to convey information; to make that information memorable. It is known that colour can be read at a greater distance with an immediacy not achievable through word, pattern or shape. The choice of colour is significant when conveying information. Food and drink labelling is a good example. The appeal of a product is usually triggered by the colours used and can encapsulate a whole definition of its properties. For example, a brown bottle indicates a greater strength of beer. Dark labels indicate rich, or strongly-flavoured foods, while light labels imply delicacy and subtlety of flavour.

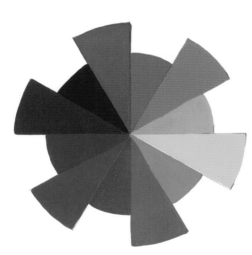

Creating secondary and tertiary colours
Secondary colours are made when two primaries are blended together in equal quantities. Yellow and red make orange, yellow and blue make green, and red and blue make violet. Tertiary colours are made when a primary and secondary are mixed together. As subtler tones, they are responsible for the overall warmth or coolness in a design, and include yellowy oranges, greeny blues, and bluey violets. Their position on the colour wheel is between the primaries and secondaries.

Making colour scales using the opaque medium of gouache can help to develop your understanding of colour theory and enable you to use it effectively in your work. When the primary, yellow, is added to its fellow primary, red, the resultant colour is orange, its secondary. Each of the primaries, red, yellow and blue can be mixed accordingly to produce a scale of colour gradation. As the purity of colour is reduced, the result is increasingly neutralized. A colour mixed with its complement creates a new, darker 'shade'

of the colour. By adding white, a 'tint' of the colour is produced. Tints and shades make ideal greys and are more natural than the mix of black and white. With the purity of saturated colour as their base, these greys will naturally harmonize when used with mixes of these colours. Alter the balance of colour when mixing these tints and shades by varying their quantities. Create these scales across a double page spread of an A3 sketchbook. Also, try making your own colour wheel, as illustrated on the facing page.

Squeeze paints onto a porcelain plate or shop-bought palette. Gouache should not be over diluted. Mix it to the consistency of single cream to keep its colour opaque and flat and its texture matt. Too much water will cause the paint to become streaky. Always mix gouache well before use and in sufficient quantities for the job in hand.

Primary blends

Yellow to red

Yellow to blue

Red to blue

Secondary blends

Orange to blue

Green to orange

Blue to green

Drawing into design

The exotic plant species housed in botanical gardens provide perfect subject matter for making drawings that can be developed into a design. Learning to source reference material at first hand and reorganize it clearly and methodically is vital for any graphic designer. Good subject matter is essential for gaining these skills, and the strong shapes, contrasting textures and deep, saturated colours of horticultural specimens are an excellent starting point.

Although many professionals design almost exclusively using computers, there are still very good reasons to learn and use drawing skills. By looking carefully and sketching, we absorb information about our subject. This is more likely to be remembered and recalled when needed in the future. First sketches alone are rarely refined enough for a design, and a stage of editing is usually necessary. Editing enables you to simplify the drawing to help the picture to convey its intention quickly and effectively.

Stylization

In developing a series of drawings or paintings, scale, composition, colour, texture and contrast are all addressed through a logical process of refinement. The final product should be dynamic, eye-catching, simplified and generally 'stylized'. Stylization occurs most often within illustration, and this exercise is an introduction to the practice of an illustrator. The chief elements are arranged in a specific way, using selective techniques and materials, to produce a clear and concise

1 | First studies are made with chalk pastel, which has good covering qualities and colour.

2 | Even at this stage selecting only the main shapes and blooms is important, saving time and giving focus.

3 | This tissue paper and PVA glue collage helps to reduce the form of the bloom to coloured shapes without losing the various textures.

4 | *Gouache has opaque properties and a dense saturation so one colour can be laid solidly over another – much like printing colours.*

5 | *The colours used were a bold combination of primaries, secondaries, tertiaries and even achromatic greys.*

6 | *Colour is a powerful tool in the hands of a good designer; with a different colour palette, the drawing remains the same but the emotional response is quite different.*

interpretation of the original piece. Stylized works often move a step beyond what has been observed in reality. Unnecessary detail may be omitted or colours changed, in order that, after this manipulation, the intended meaning of the piece is fully understood. Pictorial logos are a good example of this.

WORKING TIPS

- Experiment in the initial stages to create wider design possibilities.
- Use an A3 or A2 bound sketchbook when out gathering source material.
- Mix plenty of colour when using gouache. It should have the consistency of single cream.
- Use as many colours as necessary to convey the correct graphic message.
- Solve any visual problems on paper first. Leave nothing to chance.

7 | *Continued cropping, editing and element selection is important. A viewfinder made from two cardboard 'L' shapes is a useful tool.*

8 | *Editing out the main flower forces the eye to interpret the picture from less information. Even with very few clues, the meaning is still clear.*

9 | *Other cropped variations reveal the subtleties of editing, and just how dynamic alternatives can be.*

Visual literacy

Graphic design is basically a form of communication, and generally words and images are combined to communicate information clearly. However, images alone are particularly effective as a universal means of communication, often crossing barriers that the spoken and written word cannot. In its purest and most incisive form, graphic design can transmit complex messages simply using signs and symbols, which have been learned, that are quickly understood or are instantly recognizable.

Effective communication is bold, often televisual or multi-media based, and we have learned to recognize and understand highly sophisticated levels of information in the blink of an eye. Training the brain to respond at such levels is key, and billboards, corporate branding and symbolism, advertising and information media all utilize our response to visual prompts.

The essentials of a good symbol

Before you start to create your own signs and symbols, it is helpful to look at universal symbols, and consider what it is that makes them powerful, appealing, informative and attractive. It is interesting to note that there are cultural variations for many universal symbols. In a world where the Internet and other forms of mass communication make it increasingly important to communicate clearly across cultural and language barriers, it is reassuring to see these differences exist. A good symbol is one that communicates its message clearly despite slight variations from country to country. The green man on a pedestrian crossing is a good example, his basic style and shape might vary slightly around the world, but his message is still completely clear.

Signs and symbols

Each of the eight signs illustrated here is instantly recognizable. The underlying message is always understood becausse it is explained visually in the simplest of pictorial terms. Consider why you think each one is successful. Do you think we have learned to understand each of these symbols, or would someone seeing them for the first time immediately understand what each one means?

 EXERCISE

Choose a common object as the basis for creating a simple symbol that could be universally understood. For example, think of a tree or a specific public building and create a symbol to represent it that is instantly understood by all who see it. Simplicity is key to the success of this exercise. Test your symbols on others to gauge your success. Then take a familiar traffic sign, or a well-known symbol and alter it by adding, subtracting, recolouring or redrawing its core elements, so that the viewer is forced to think about it in a new way. Can the message still be understood despite the changes? Show your designs to other people to find out if they work.

No entry *This sign is always circular and red so that it is not easy to ignore. The wide, white band across the middle represents a crossing out or a bar, blocking the way forward.*

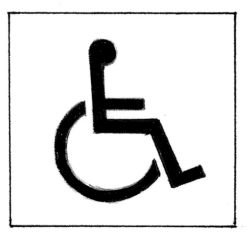

Disabled *This is a curious symbol. The figure sits back in the hub of a wheel. No more detail of the wheelchair is included but as peculiar as it seems, this symbol works and is now firmly fixed in the common psyche.*

Taxi *The word 'taxi' is internationally recognized as is this symbol. The block on the roof could be mistaken for a police car light, but in symbolic terms, light flashes would be shown with radiating strokes.*

Toilets *Usually seen as part of a pair, we all recognize this simple figure in a dress as a woman and know that it usually indicates toilets. The whole meaning of this clear code could be broken by the inclusion of say, a dog!*

First Aid *Whether a red cross on a white background or a white cross on a green background, this is a universal symbol for medical assistance.*

One way *The arrow is a strong authoritative symbol and demands attention with its definite vertical stroke. Sitting on a blue background, it is not easily missed and urges you to move in one direction only.*

Telephone *In the same way that trains are often represented as steam locomotives of a bygone age, the old pre-digital, bell-dial phone is still used to indicate a public telephone.*

No smoking *This is more illustrative, even showing a simplified form of ash and smoke. The red diagonal stroke through the picture leaves us in no doubt that the activity is not allowed.*

Developing and expanding creative thought

How do you draw the wind? Certainly, it can be felt and its power experienced through its influence upon the physical world, but its visual representation poses a certain problem to the visual artist. The example exercise that follows shows how you can progress from first ideas through a connective sequence to a creative outcome, which could still be developed in a number of ways.

The purpose of setting yourself this type of exercise is not to produce the most beautiful artwork, rather to follow a logical and sequential train of thought, employing appropriate media, to illustrate the movement and characteristics of wind. Before you begin it is fundamental that you have a clear idea in mind of what it is that you are attempting to achieve. The best design outcomes usually conclude after much deliberation. In this case small group discussion set the project in motion.

Brainstorming

In this example a large sheet of paper was laid on the table and ideas were bounced around the group before being noted down on the paper with a broad, felt marker pen. Verbalized thoughts were written onto the sheets. Some words emerged as a result of conscious thought, others by association. Out of wind, came breeze, gust, cyclone, hurricane, whirlwind and twister, and out of this came plughole, slipstream and vortex.

The first visuals were an investigation of the idea of the plughole, but this served only to eliminate the idea as too tenuous a link with wind.

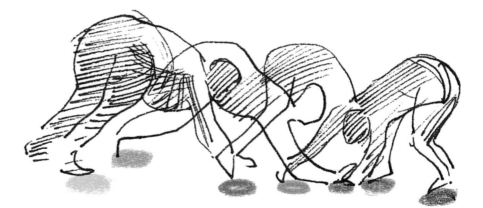

Later a game of human movement called 'Twister' provoked the exciting idea of **personifying the wind** and its movement through the movement of twisting figures.

The colours of **blue, red, yellow and green** from the circles on the playing mat were incorporated into the scheme.

Providing an excellent basis for life drawing too, the room was set up and the group played for the afternoon, providing opportunity for **spontaneous, figure studies** in a range of media.

Further **marks to convey movement** were tried in a range of media, from flowing pencil lines through line and wash spirals and directional cross-hatching. The twister colours were employed where appropriate.

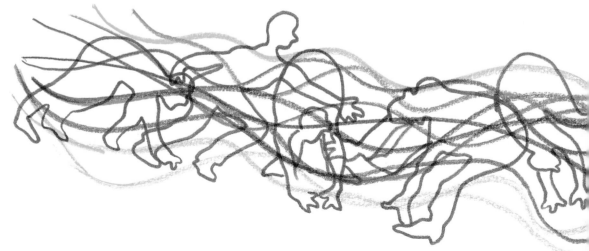

Building on the success of the figure studies, **white, linear shapes** were traced from the watercolour drawings using blue felt-tip pens. This clean-edged, graphic approach produced a highly animated line of inter-linking bodies.

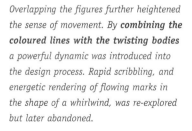

Overlapping the figures further heightened the sense of movement. By **combining the coloured lines with the twisting bodies** a powerful dynamic was introduced into the design process. Rapid scribbling, and energetic rendering of flowing marks in the shape of a whirlwind, was re-explored but later abandoned.

Final image

In the end, it was decided to return to a more formalized
solution of portraying the wind carrying the figures
around the directional path of its movement. The
contrast of the whiteness of the figures against the blue
background provided increased clarity. The contour marks
running around the figures made reference to both the
movement of the air and also to the presence of isobars
during a low-pressure weather front as depicted on a
meteorological chart. This project's open-endedness is
deliberate. Metamorphosis for an object to turn into
another through imagery transformation would have
been a good continuation of the idea, revealing a strong
resolve into the formation of swirling, abstract elements.

The structure of type

Where it was once the job of the designer to create a layout as a guide to those who would set the type in hot metal, computerized design now allows the designer to send finished layouts with final pictures and type in place straight to the printing press. It is therefore essential for any graphic designer to have an intimate knowledge of type, its structure and form and to be aware of typographic rules that have been proven successful for over 500 years of use.

The importance of typography

Typography is a subtle craft, in which the smallest mistake can appear as a glaring error even to the untrained eye. Unlike the spoken word, which quickly passes and is forgotten, printed type has the potential to survive for hundreds of years. The adoption of good habits and a healthy respect for type characters and fonts is a good starting point for anyone wishing to practice graphic design.

Parts of a line of type
The flat top and bottom of a lower-case character sit between the mean line and baseline and this is called the x-height. The curved tops and bottoms of the p, o and g, extend beyond these lines, so that they appear visually to fit the x-height. The size of the type is defined by the distance between the baseline and that of the line below it.

1	Ascender line	**5**	Descender	**8**	Cap line
2	Base line	**6**	Ascender	**9**	Mean line
3	Ascender height	**7**	X-height	**10**	Descender line
4	Cap height				

Type families

All licensed, commercial fonts (type alphabet set) are available in a number of styles and weights, usually roman (sometimes known as plain or book), italic (sometimes called oblique), bold and bold italic. For flexible working, it is best to choose a broad type family rather than use many different fonts. The sans serif font Helvetica Neue has a vast type family (shown below), containing many intermediary weights rarely found in most type families. As well as Light, the font provides a further option of Ultra, and in addition to Medium and Bold, Heavy and Black are provided. Plantin, in contrast, has a much smaller type family of only nine variations.

A problem with non-commercial fonts, such as those that have free usage or are Internet downloads, is that they often have only one weight, and are therefore of limited use. Another problem is that font sizes may not be standardized.

Helvetica Neue type family

Ultra Light	Roman	**Heavy**
Ultra Light Italic	*Italic*	***Heavy Italic***
Light	**Medium**	**Heavy Condensed**
Light Italic	***Medium Italic***	***Heavy Condensed Oblique***
Light Condensed	Medium Condensed	**Black**
Light Condensed Oblique	*Medium Condensed Oblique*	**Black Condensed**
Thin	**Bold**	***Black Condensed Oblique***
Thin Italic	***Bold Italic***	***Black Italic***

Plantin type family

Plain	***Bold Italic***	*Light Italic*
Bold	*Italic*	Semibold
Bold Condensed	Light	*Semibold Italic*

Choosing a font

Letterforms are more than simply characters to be read, additional information arises out of the associations that are attached to various styles of type. For example, you can easily see the difference in the character of the typefaces used in a Wild West 'wanted' poster and those used for a traditional wedding invitation. Successful designing with type is all about making the most of those associations to make your visual point.

The first thing that you do when you receive copy (text) for a design job is to read it for sense. Whether it a 20,000-word book or a single word logo, ask yourself 'what does this actually mean?' If you can answer this question yourself, how can you hope to convey this successfully to others? The typographic treatment sets the overall mood of a piece; clean, traditional choices for straight information delivery may suit a corporate report, whereas, more funky stylized fonts might work better for a poster promoting modern dance. The huge range of typefaces available on the market is almost overwhelming. You can make a bit of sense of this by applying broad categories to fonts according to function, as many type foundries do as a matter of course.

Weight and style

Type families are constructed to provide a complete set of weights that share a strong family resemblance. Helvetica Ultra Light works well with Helvetica Ultra Black because they are siblings, arising from the same basic forms. As a rule of thumb, any design layout from a large book to a matchbox, calls for no more than three font families throughout. You can use the range of tonal weights within families to extend your scope, lending depth and selective emphasis to your typography.

Initial choices
The four primary weights of roman, bold, italic and bold italic have some long held traditional uses in writing; for example, a quotation is usually set in italics. Beyond strict proper usage, choices of weight are largely discretionary. Within narrative text or dialogue, selective variations in weight can alter the particular emphasis of a word or phrase, enriching the meaning. Where roman type is straightforwardly conversational, italics might be broadly thought of as whispering or pausing, and bold can perhaps be regarded as shouting.

The overall typographic treatment of a piece will usually be yours to decide. However, in some cases, typographic choices will come directly from the client. For example, a publisher will often provide a hard copy (print out) that has been marked for typesetting. Alternatively, text supplied on disk may have been pre-formatted by an editor.

light

bold

italic

Serifed body fonts, *often called book fonts, are designed for easy legibility and fluid readability. They are best suited for setting large amounts of copy.*

abcdefghijklmnopqrstuvwxyx
abcdefghijklmnopqrstuvwxyz

abcdefghijklmnopqrstuvwxyz
abcdefghijklmnopqrstuvwxyz

Sans serif fonts *Typefaces without serifs present a clean, modern look that is particularly good for display copy (18 points and above) but also suitable for body copy*

Antique fonts *These fonts have a long history and can be used to evoke a period feel.*

abcdefghijklmnopqrstuvwxyz
abcdefghijklmnopqrstuvwxyz

abcdefghijklmnopqrstuvwxyz
ABCDEFGHIJKLMNOPQRST

Decorative fonts *These include highly decorated and really eccentric fonts, often with very specific uses and rarely appropriate for more than three words at a time.*

Script fonts, *which resemble handwriting, can be subdivided into traditional scripts that look as though they were produced by a quill pen and those that mimic modern styles of handwriting.*

abcdefghijklmnopqrstuvwxyz
abcdefghijklmnopqrstuvwxyz

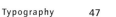

Symbol fonts *are composed of graphic icons to provide embellishments to text. These are sometimes created to complement a specific font.*

Drawing letterforms by hand

Just as your visual sense of form and function is enhanced by drawing the human figure from life, designing your own letterforms improves your ability to work with type. The sophisticated art of creating new typefaces can be a life's work, but even making the most basic attempt to fashion a functional alphabet will sharpen your design skills.

From the roots of calligraphy in illustrated manuscripts to modern-day font design, a pattern of underlying structures and scales has developed to which all durable typefaces conform. With 26 basic characters, not to mention the punctuation marks and additional symbols that form a typeface, the seemingly endless variations between faces arise from the subtlest differences in form.

Begin by drawing a single letterform on a grid. Experiment with its shape and proportions until you find it aesthetically pleasing, then draw its upper- or lower-case companion.

Using the guidance provided in the diagrams on page 44 as a reference, apply a framework of gridlines to your letterforms. Each structural decision in relation to your first letterform will describe the fundamental rules for the entire typeface. For example, the shapes of curves, angles of uprights and obliques and the ratios of internal strokes to crossbars within characters should be consistent for each character of the typeface. The ultimate aim is to arrive at an alphabet whose letterforms enjoy harmonious relationships when in sequence.

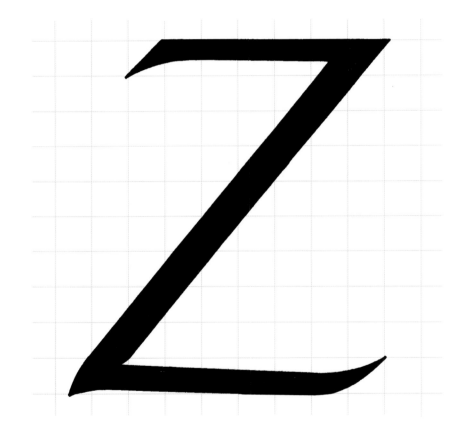

*This elegant Z is a good **starting point** for our serifed typeface. The lower arm lifts gently away from the baseline to accentuate a smoothly tapering lower serif, suggestive of a brush or quill stroke. The harder angle of the upper serif mirrors that of the diagonal stem, which is subtly thicker than the horizontals.*

By exploring the **underlying geometric forms** and rules of each character, you can apply them universally to build a consistent typeface. In this sans serif example, the important ratio of letterform height to stroke width is investigated. The position and proportions of ascenders and descenders is also examined.

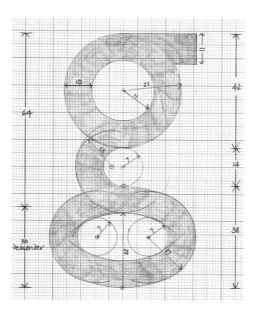

Two points set at a 15-degree angle from each other form the central rotational axis for the circles that create both **top and bottom loops** of the capital B. The original curves are flattened top and bottom to lend definition, and adjusted within to give a consistency of width where the loops join the vertical bar (the stoke width of these connections is about one third of the main stem). Added last, the serifs mirror the final curves in opposition.

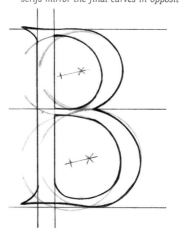

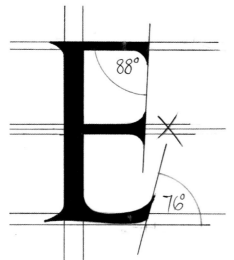

The letter E can be formed from the combination of L and F. In this example the final extent of the middle arm aligns to the serif angle of the top arm. The movement away from an exact right angle adds shape and interest. The middle arm sits exactly on the midline at half the stroke width of the vertical bar, the bottom arm sweeps along the baseline in a gentle curve moving the eye fluidly to the next character.

The capital Q is created through the addition of a tail to the O. Finding a **common angle for decenders** is achieved by first drawing a right angle from the outer edges of the letterform and taking your angle axis from there. Q must be primarily suited to sitting well with its usual companion U, the extended flourish in the example above is designed to flow beautifully beneath the rounded underside of the subsequent U, accentuating the curve.

Styling text

Good typography, especially within body copy, often passes unnoticed as the information leaps from the page quickly and cleanly. However, this does not mean that your efforts are wasted; the reader's ease of reading demonstrates that you have done your job well. Conversely, bad typography is memorable and intrusive. You will over time develop your own typographic preferences, but your choices need to be founded on a clear understanding of underlying principles.

Lorem ipsum dolor sit amet, consectetuer adipiscing elit, sed diam nonummy nibh euismod tincidunt ut laoreet dolore magna erat volutpat. Ut wisi enim ad minim veniam, quis nostrud exerci tation ullamcorper.

The sans serif Helvetica Neue Light set in 14pt on 16pt leading is a highly legible choice for body copy.

Type size

Body copy forms the main bulk of any text. Its primary function is to deliver information, so legibility is the most crucial consideration. A point (pt) is the usual measurement for type and is equivalent to $\frac{1}{72}$ of an inch or approximately 0.351mm. Type that is smaller than 7pt is difficult to read and type that is smaller than 3pt is utterly illegible. The size range for body copy in a book or magazine article should be between 8pt and 14pt. In general 9pt or 10pt are the most practical choices.

Serif or sans serif?

A serif font is easier to read over long passages than a sans serif font and is therefore often chosen for designs incorporating high volumes of body copy, such as novels and newspapers. However, a sans serif font is frequently perceived as being more modern.

Body copy should always be set in upper- and lower-case because the irregular shapes are rich with cues that improve legibility. Upper-case (capital) letters are uniform in height and lack diversity of form, which impairs reading. Upper-case text also consumes about a third more space than the equivalent in lower-case.

Leading

Leading is the vertical space separating baselines in text and is traditionally measured in points. The term is derived from the days of setting type in hot metal, when strips of lead were used to add space between lines. Where leading is set to the same point size of the copy, it is referred to as 'set solid'. Although text set solid is often entirely legible, large blocks of copy set solid are tiring to read. Where possible, you should add at least 2 points of leading to your body copy. For example, for 9pt type choose 11pt leading. Leading of more than this amount is often aesthetically pleasing if your design can accommodate it. If leading is set below the type size, ascenders and descenders crash, which looks unsightly and affects legibility.

Lorem ipsum dolor sit amet, consectetuer adipiscing elit, sed diam nonummy nibh euismod tincidunt ut laoreet dolore magna erat volutpat. Ut wisi enim ad minim veniam, quis nostrud exerci tation ullamcorper. Lorem ipsum dolor sit amet

*Setting copy on **leading of less than the type size** is suitable only for special effects (Plantin 10/8pt).*

Lorem ipsum dolor sit amet, consectetuer adipiscing elit, sed diam nonummy nibh euismod tincidunt ut laoreet dolore magna erat volutpat. Ut wisi enim ad minim veniam, quis nostrud exerci tation ullamcorper. Lorem ipsum dolor sit amet

*Copy **set solid** in a serif face is often perfectly legible, but is tiring to read in large amounts (Plantin 10/10pt).*

Lorem ipsum dolor sit amet, consectetuer adipiscing elit, sed diam nonummy nibh euismod tincidunt ut laoreet dolore magna erat volutpat. Ut wisi enim ad minim veniam, quis nostrud exerci tation ullamcorper. Lorem ipsum dolor sit amet

Two points of additional leading can give more spaciousness to your design (Plantin 10/12pt).

As you read this passage you may find that you make slower progress than your normal reading speed, because of the over long line length the eye has far to travel and struggles to quickly find the beginning of each new line. As you read this passage you may find that you make slower progress than your normal reading speed, because of the over long line length the eye has far to travel and and struggles

It is generally agreed that about 70 characters (10 to12 words) is the maximum line length for comfortable reading, which is why columns are often used for wide pages. It is generally agreed that about 70 characters (10 to12 words) is the maximum line length for comfortable reading, which is why columns are often

Measure

The width of the text column is also a critical factor in the legibilty of type. A wide measure can be tiring to read because the eye cannot easily scan from the end of one line to the start of the next. A short measure can also disrupt readability and can lead to unsightly line breaks. The optimum line length for body copy is 60–70 characters.

Alignment

Alignment refers to the arrangement of lines of text in relation to the page margins. There are four dominant styles illustrated below.
• Ranged left (ragged right), in which the text is aligned to the left-hand margin is most common, legible and aesthetically pleasing (see facing page, below right). The majority of your text should be aligned right unless you have a sound reason to do otherwise.
• Ranged right (ragged left) is hard to read at speed because the eye struggles to find the start

of each new line. However, it can be stylish for short blocks of text.
• Centred text, in which the text is centred on each line, should be used sparingly. While appropriate for display type and headings, it should not be used for body copy.
• Justified text, ranging to both the left and right margins, can be a neat solution. However, it can create excessive spaces between words and may require hyphenation.

Equally, overly short lines create a flickering effect, which may severely limit legibility. Equally, overly short lines create a flickering effect, which may severely limit legibility.

Equally, overly short lines create a flickering effect, which may severely limit legibility. Equally, overly short lines create a flickering effect, which may severely limit legibility.

Lorem ipsum dolor sit amet, consectetuer adipiscing elit, sed diam nonummy nibh euismod tincidunt ut laoreet dolore magna erat volutpat. Ut wisi enim ad minim veniam, quis nostrud exerci tation ullamcorper. Lorem ipsum dolor sit amet

Justified setting (Plantin 10/12pt).

Lorem ipsum dolor sit amet, consectetuer adipiscing elit, sed diam nonummy nibh euismod tincidunt ut laoreet dolore magna erat volutpat. Ut wisi enim ad minim veniam, quis nostrud exerci tation ullamcorper. Lorem ipsum dolor sit amet

Centred setting (Plantin 10/12pt).

Lorem ipsum dolor sit amet, consectetuer adipiscing elit, sed diam nonummy nibh euismod tincidunt ut laoreet dolore magna erat volutpat. Ut wisi enim ad minim veniam, quis nostrud exerci tation ullamcorper. Lorem ipsum dolor sit amet

Ranged right setting (Plantin 10/12pt).

More type-styling choices

Once you have made the major decisions on type styling, there are many other choices you will need to make to create a harmonious overall design. A sound design structure arises from solid internal logic – each element speaking the same language albeit in different voices. Even when your design is entirely defined, there are common visual pitfalls that may occur at layout stage, ruining an otherwise good design. Paying close attention to these typesetting finishing touches elevates a good design to excellence.

100 per cent scaling

170 per cent horizontal scaling

60 per cent horizontal scaling

Typographical fine tuning
By using the opportunities offered by page-layout programs for fine-tuning the proportions of the letterforms and their spatial relationships, you can create typesetting that is both legible and aesthetically pleasing. Take the trouble to experiment with these aspects of type specification so that you can become familiar with the range of possibilities.

Horizontal and vertical scales are set to 100 per cent by default. You can stretch or compress the letterforms along the x or y axis respectively by adjusting the scale values. This can be useful for display setting.

0 tracking

+10 tracking

–10 tracking

*A **Ligature** is a character formed by joining two or more separate characters. For typesetting body text it is preferable to use such characters when they are available. They can be specified individually or automatically by your page layout program.*

***Kerning** describes the process of adapting the horizontal space between specific characters. The term arises from 'kern', which means the projecting part of a piece of type. Kerning adjustments are most commonly required in display type when the standard space between certain characters creates an ugly space.*

***Tracking** is the horizontal space between characters in a line of type. By increasing the tracking value you can create greater 'airiness' in your typesetting. Reducing the amount of tracking makes for a denser effect.*

Paragraph formatting

Text styles are not simply defined by font and weight; paragraph styling or 'formatting' also has a part to play. For example, you will also have to decide whether to include a line space before each new paragraph or whether simply to indent the first. If you choose the latter scheme, it is traditional to start indentation only after the opening paragraph for all those subsequent within a section. Some other formatting considerations are colour, shade, space above and/or below paragraph headings and the use of graphic elements within the typographic structure.

You may define your paragraph breaks by either indention or by a space interval. If you elect indention, the standard width of a paragraph indent is between 1 and 3 ems. You may find that your software's default tab setting is too long; however, all professional DTP packages allow you to define your own tabulation on a paragraph-by-paragraph basis. In fact, self-defined tabulation simplifies the whole typesetting process from body text to bullets, especially as you can embed this formatting information in your style sheets.

Heading hierarchies

Any text-heavy design project, such as a book or annual report, requires a sound and consistent typographic scheme to be successful. When you approach a new brief, read the given text carefully to ascertain the differing types of information that it contains. Even if your copy is supplied totally unformatted you can still see that the data (whatever it may be) breaks down into parts on a recognizable scale of importance. For example, section titles, titles that begin paragraphs, subtitles within paragraphs and body copy. Editors and designers usually give a specific name

*Copy may be marked up by hand on a print out or, increasingly commonly as files are exchanged digitally, you may find **typesetting instructions** embedded in the text supplied by an author or editor.*

or letter to each varying style of information within a given document. For example, you might have chapter titles, A heads, B heads, C heads and D heads in descending order of impact throughout your design.

The titles and headings are your display text and you may elect to treat them entirely differently from the body text, although all headings within a piece should belong to a single type family, with depth and contrast arising from a scale of size and weight. Headings may either complement or counterbalance the body copy but unless the choices are aesthetically sympathetic with each other then the design will not work well.

TIP

Once you have set all your styles and formatting, it is excellent practice to create style sheets in your DTP application. This facility allows you to apply styles to selected text with a single 'click'. Using style sheets has the additional advantage that once styles are assigned, you can change your mind at any point and alter a particular style throughout the document.

```
[[PP026-027]]

( A HEAD )
Creative thinking

( INTRO TEXT )
Creative visual thinking is a process that is usually best approached
as a problem-solving discipline. In other words to achieve a feasible
solution, creative thinking and practical problem-solving need to
happen at the same time. In order to formulate your ideas and communicate
them clearly, you need to take a systematic approch. It is helpful to
break the process down into five stages.

( B HEAD )
Types of creative thinking

( BODY TEXT )
Groups of ideas — 'concepts' — are the creative solutions to design
problems. Concepts and ideas cannot be forced: and solutions can often
be stumbled upon by accident. Ideas may occur unexpectedly in the
middle of the night or under the pressure of a morning shower.

( new para )
However, once a basic concept is in place, there should be sound
reasons for your choice of imagery, colour, typography and composition.
From this point, the elements chosen must reflect the objectives of the
brief and communicate their message clearly. There are a number of
helpful methods for stimulating creative thinking that will help you
formulate your ideas clearly and enable you to present them visually.

( C HEAD )
Free thinking
This is also known as brainstorming, and it involves making a list of
anything, however tenuous or silly it might seem, that comes to mind
concerning a subject. The main thing is not to worry about what anyone
might think, and to open your mind and think as freely as possible.
```

Widows and orphans

Some typographical adjustments can only be made editorially in the latter stages of layout, including the removal of widows and orphans. A widow is a very short line that has been left on its own at the end of a paragraph, column or page. An orphan (even worse) is a single word on a line of its own. Orphans look terrible, especially when they appear at the top of a column or worse, at the top of a page. Remove orphans and widows through careful adjustment of line endings. It takes sharp eyes to spot these typographical problems and you need to remember that the most minor amendment to copy can produce a problem of this kind so a final check is always required.

Rivers

In typography, a river is a visual phenomenon where the spaces between words accidentally align horizontally or diagonally, creating distracting white lines through the text area. The effect is only a problem where the alignment runs through more than three lines, at which point legibility is at risk. Rivers occur most commonly in justified text and must be corrected if found. Simply adjusting the shortest word from a long line in the problem area up or down a line usually eliminates the river.

Hyphenation

A naturally hyphenated word (for example, yo-yo) should break immediately after the hyphen if it splits across a line. When a long word is automatically hyphenated to break over two lines, check for legibility and, if necessary, select your own hyphenation point. You can obtain a dictionary of correct word breaks if you are not working in conjunction with an editor who can advise on hyphenation. Many designers turn off the automatic hyphenation option in their page layout program, making subtle line-end adjustments manually to correct any awkward spaces that this might leave.

Exerci tation ullamcorper suscipit lobortis nisl ut aliquip ex ea commodo consequat. Duis voluptat autem vel eum iriure dolor in hendrerit in vulputate velit esse molestie consequat, vel illum dolore eu feugiat nulla facilisis at vero eros et accumsan iusto odio.

Dignissim qui blandit praesent luptatum zzril delenit augue duis dolore te feugait nulla facilisi. Lorem ipsum dolor sit amet, consectuer adipiscing elit, sed diam nonummy nibh euismod tincidunt ut laoreet dolore magna aliquam erat volupat. Ut wisi enim ad minim veniam, quis nostrud vel illumium

*A **widow** is a short line at the end of a paragraph.*

odio.

Dignissim qui blandit praesent luptatum zzril delenit augue duis dolore te feugait nulla facilisi. Lorem ipsum dolor sit amet, consectetuer adipiscing elit, sed diam nonummy nibh euismod tincidunt ut laoreet dolore magna aliquam erat volutpat. Exerci tation ullamcorper suscipit lobortis nisl ut aliquip ex ea commodo consequat. Duis autem vel eum iriure dolor in hendrerit in vulputate velit esse molestie consequat, vel illum dolore eu feugait nulla facilisis at vero eros et accumsan et iusto odio. Ut wisi enim ad minim veniam, quis nostrud aliquar

*An **orphan** is a single word on a line. The worst instances occur at the top of a column.*

For example, you can see small rivers in these three identical typeset lines. For example, you can see small rivers in these three identical typeset lines. For example, you can see small rivers in these three identical typeset lines.

For example, you can see small rivers in these three identical typeset lines. For example, you can see small rivers in these three identical typeset lines. For example, you can see small rivers in these three identical typeset lines. For example, you

***Rivers in text** can be adjusting by taking a short word in the area affected over to the next line.*

Line-ending adjustments

Make careful line-ending adjustments to address rivers, orphans, widows and bad hyphenation. To be thorough you can also adjust the lines where you feel that the distance between the longest and shortest line of a column makes for uneasy reading. The simplest correction is to knock a short word over to the next line using a soft return (alt-enter on your keyboard) to amend the problem. Unlike a hard return, which creates a new paragraph, a soft return retains the identity and styling characteristics of the paragraph within which it occurs.

Tracking and horizontal scaling can also be used to take words back or over to the next line.

You can track a line between −2 and +2 points from the body setting before the spacing looks incongruous. Horizontal scaling can be used within the range of 97 to 102 per cent before the typeface noticeably distorts; exceeding this range will make the font appear to be of another weight entirely. A combination of tracking and horizontal scaling is acceptable within the given limits. If you assign, say, +2 points of tracking to all of your body text from the start, then you have more flexibility with line endings, increasing your comfortable adjustment range to between −3.5 and +1.5 points. Justified text obeys none of these rules and is much harder to correct, which may deter you from choosing this styling.

Ens and ems

An en space occupies the same width as a lower-case letter n and an em space inhabits that of an m. En spaces are the standard distance between words. En and em dashes (or rules) are horizontal dashes of the same lengths. A hyphen (see facing page) is the shortest dash available and is used is to break words between lines or for naturally hyphenated words. An en rule is used to express a range and in this case is set closed up to the figures in question. In UK-style typesetting a spaced en rule is used as a dash in punctuation. However, in American publications a closed up em rule is preferred for this usage.

"Quotes may be styled to attract attention"

*A **quote 'pulled out'** from the body text can make an eye-catching graphic feature.*

TIP

You can race through your document assigning correct dashes by using the Find/Replace function of your DTP package replacing standard en rules with em rules or visa versa, as appropriate. Working at high magnification will make this task even easier.

Bullet points

Bullet points are really no more than a fancy list. Select a symbol font that is in sympathy with your body type for the actual bullet. This will allow you to achieve a more interesting graphic shape than is possible with a bullet from the same font, and will allow a larger bullet in the same point size as your body copy without affecting leading values. A poorly designed bullet point butts up to the paragraph in which it sits as if the information is no different from the body copy, thus rendering the treatment ineffective.

Quotations

A long quotation should be set as a separate paragraph with a little space to separate it from the body copy. You can also incorporate additional styling features. A quotation is usually italicized and looks best if slightly indented from the left-hand margin. If there is enough space, you might want to indent equally from the right-hand margin, too. Sometimes quotations become more prominent graphic elements. The may be pulled out from the copy and enlarged and styled to draw one's attention, for example, to a magazine article.

- Lorem ipsum dolor sit amet, consectetuer adipiscing elit, sed diam nonummy nibh euismod tincidunt.
- Ut wisi enim ad minim veniam, quis nostrud exercitation ullamcorper.
- Lorem ipsum dolor sit amet, consectetuer adipiscing elit, sed diam nonummy nibh euismod tincidunt.

*These **standard bullet points** are set so that the second and subsequent lines align with the bullet at the left-hand margin.*

- Lorem ipsum dolor sit amet, consectetuer adipiscing elit, sed diam nonummy nibh euismod.
- Ut wisi enim ad minim veniam, quis nostrud exercitation ullamcorper.
- Lorem ipsum dolor sit amet, consectetuer adipiscing elit, sed diam nonummy nibh euismod.

*In this neater treatment, the second and subsequent lines are **aligned with the left edge of the first character** of the text.*

- Lorem ipsum dolor sit amet, consectetuer adipiscing elit, sed diam.
- Ut wisi enim ad minim veniam, quis nostrud exercitation ullamcorper.
- Lorem ipsum dolor sit amet, consectetuer adipiscing elit, sed diam

*A symbol font – Zapf Dingbats – has been used to create **square bullets centred on the cap height**. For greater spaciousness there is a line space between each item.*

Text as tone

The best device for understanding how typography operates tonally is to take a good squint at the printed page. This will help you see the variations in light and dark. These tonal differences influence the impact of each graphic element, the stronger the contrast the greater the weight of that object. Using a wide range of tones will lead to greater flexibility and interest in your designs.

As the letterforms take about one-third of the occupied space, you might consider normally leaded, fully black body copy to have a nominal shade value of around 35 per cent. Light typefaces are obviously paler in tone than a Bold or Heavy face. A condensed face will also appear darker. So, when judging the tonal balance of your layout you might seek successful contrasts by, for example, using a heavy face to oppose white space and minimal image use, or by using a light face adjacent to a tonally heavy image. When placing text over an image the reverse is desirable: heavy to heavy and light to light. A thin typeface does not reverse well out of a strong solid background at body copy size because it becomes overwhelmed; similarly, chunky display faces don't generally work well on spacious, subtle or airy images.

EXERCISE

Taking the letters of your full name, rearrange them in varying sizes within one typeface and one colour, repeating the copy as often as you like. Assign different tints and gradients to the letterforms, applying backgrounds in some places and not in others. Try out transparency effects. Treat some text as display copy, another section as body copy and experiment with more as pure texture. You are not aiming at aesthetic harmony; instead try to create a piece as varied as possible in its description of space, depth, light and volume. When you are happy with your work, save and print out a copy for future reference before moving beyond monochrome and applying contrasting colours to explore how this affects your arrangement. Later reflection on the results of this exercise will help you gauge the 'mood' of individual typographic arrangements, helping you achieve designs that are both dynamic and uncluttered.

1 Different tonal values have been assigned to selected letters to create a pattern of light and dark.

2 Using colour as tone, different tints have been assigned to the tonal values selected in the previous version. As you squint at the design, you can see the different tones of the colours selected.

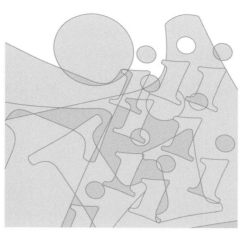

3 Using a different range of typefaces, tonal exploration has been used here to create **an illustrative effect**. The variation in the sizes and proportions of letterforms and the use of white space provides added interest.

5 Created entirely out of the lowercase 'I' of one typeface, this jumbly **texture reminiscent of landscape** is an ideal background texture. In greyscale we get perfect values for a tint background over which black body copy can be printed. Overlaying pale or reversed out text would be ineffective.

7 This dense, tonally rich image beautifully illustrates the difference in **contrast considerations** between colour modes. The strongest colour contrast in this piece is between the complementary colours blue and orange, drawing the eye towards the centre.

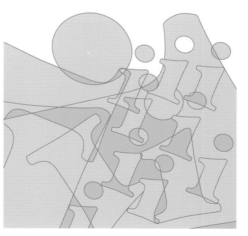

4 Colour has been incorporated into the original monochrome design. The carefully selected hues are consistent with the **tonal values** previously selected.

6 Even though this **coloured version** is graphically strong, well chosen display copy could overlay to good effect without becoming confusing, especially if a complementary colour such as a violet were chosen.

8 When **converted to monochrome** the orange becomes completely neutral, but the variation in tonal depth from the blue areas gives rich patternation, focusing the eye around the edges of the square. It would be hard to make other typographic elements combine with this texture, except perhaps very large bold display type.

Introducing the design grid

Designs love structure, and modern page layout software has been devised to help us achieve this ideal. The margins, baseline grid and guides are useful visual cues that can be turned on and off selectively to provide different structural viewpoints. When design elements align, even at a distance, the eye appreciates the balance and harmony, and is led effortlessly from one element to the next.

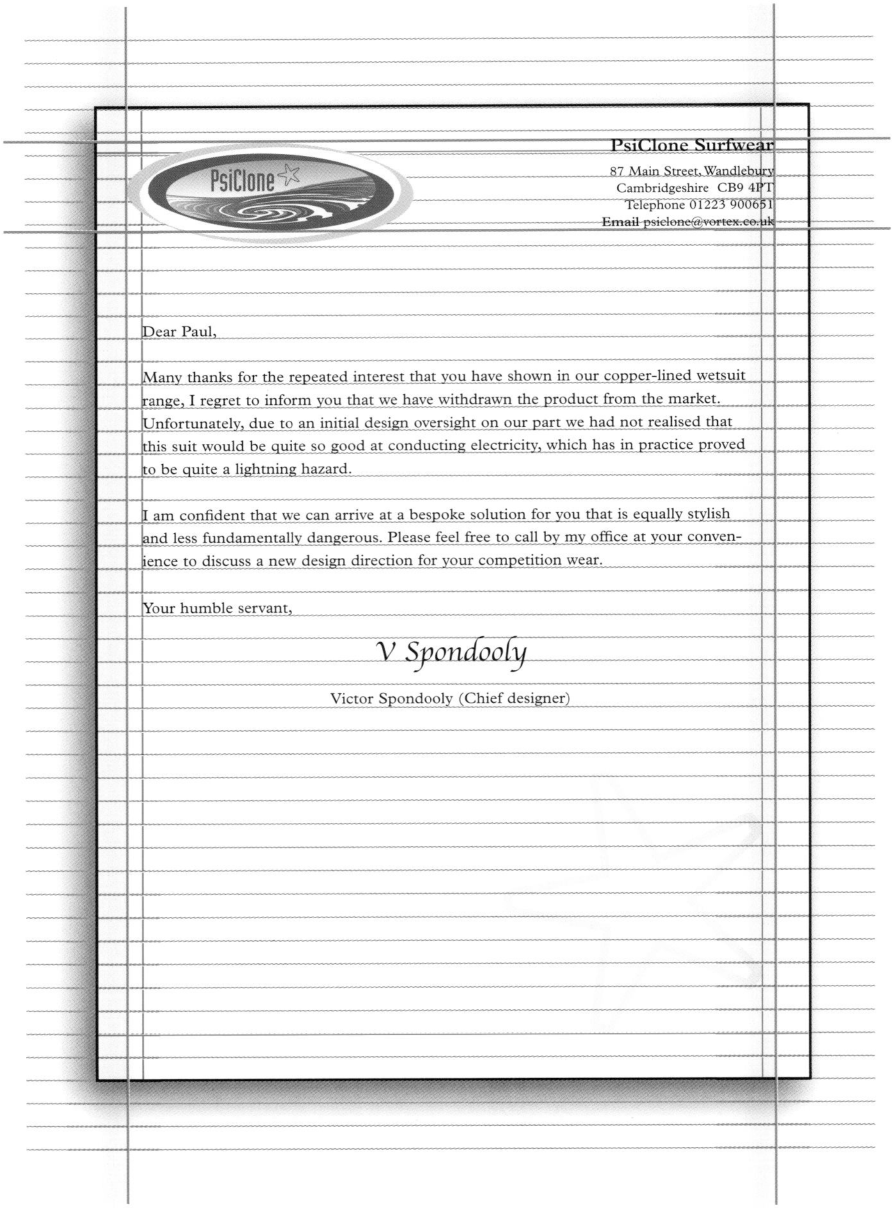

PsiClone Surfwear

87 Main Street, Wandlebury
Cambridgeshire CB9 4PT
Telephone 01223 900651
Email psiclone@vortex.co.uk

Dear Paul,

Many thanks for the repeated interest that you have shown in our copper-lined wetsuit range, I regret to inform you that we have withdrawn the product from the market. Unfortunately, due to an initial design oversight on our part we had not realised that this suit would be quite so good at conducting electricity, which has in practice proved to be quite a lightning hazard.

I am confident that we can arrive at a bespoke solution for you that is equally stylish and less fundamentally dangerous. Please feel free to call by my office at your convenience to discuss a new design direction for your competition wear.

Your humble servant,

V Spondooly

Victor Spondooly (Chief designer)

The baseline grid *reflects the leading value for the main text of your document. When you create your grid, you assign a point value for the leading and also determine where on the page the grid begins. If you 'lock' text to the baseline grid then it will adhere to the predefined baselines regardless of other styling. Locking text can limit your flexibility and adding defined space above or below locked text will simply knock a line down to the next available baseline. However, locking to the baseline is useful for quickly aligning columns of text on a page without the need for fine-tuning.*

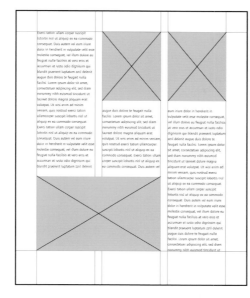

*This **simple grid** consists of a single column. Such setting is suitable for text-only publications such as novels where a more complex layout is not needed.*

*A **three-column grid** offers the possibility of placing illustrations over one, two, or three columns without disrupting the harmony of the design.*

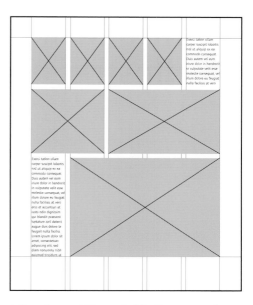

*A **five-column grid** is very flexible. Text can extend over one or two columns, allowing different types of text, such as body copy and captions, to occupy different measures.*

Margins

Margins define the borders of your document. Generous margins generally enhance a design. A bottom margin slightly deeper than the top margin creates visual balance. A layout of spreads (two or more pages side-by-side) is considered to have inside and outside margins according to which way each page faces the fold or spine. When working with a book that is to be perfect bound (having a glued spine), you must provide additional space in the inside margins to compensate for the binding. Your printer can give you a measurement for this adjustment once the full page extent is known.

Using a grid creatively

When building a grid, you can give harmony to your design by choosing a base number to work with, such as three, four or five. Don't let this number hamper your designs, but do allow it to influence your placement choices, making full use of the computer's measurement functions. For example, with base six in mind, the margins might be 12mm ($\frac{1}{2}$ in) all round with 18mm ($\frac{3}{4}$ in) for the bottom margin. An object placed on the layout, aligned left, may be pleasingly positioned 30 or 36mm (1 or 1$\frac{1}{2}$ in) from the margin. Roughly applying such a scheme leads to equilibrium and overall harmony.

T I P

Guides are optionally mobile, temporary lines that you pull out of the ruler areas of your document window. Use your guides liberally and frequently to align and arrange elements of your design.

Introducing illustration

Pictures speak an international language. They narrate without needing words. Since medieval monks painstakingly placed intricate illuminations into handwritten religious texts, illustrations, including photographs and traditional or computer-generated artwork, have enjoyed a long partnership with words. Planning for non-text elements should form an integral part of your earliest design concepts.

Illustration choices

Whether the job entails a wealth of stunning photographs, demands specially commissioned artwork, or simply needs some coloured bands or tint boxes to 'lift' otherwise visually monotonous content, the styling, commissioning and utilization of illustrative material can affect the whole character of your graphic designs. If you are responsible for styling a job, whether a book, packaging or website, the type of illustrative content will form part of the proposal you make to your client. You will have to decide whether to use photography or hand-drawn artwork, and in what style. You will also need to work out the balance between text and illustration, if this hasn't been predetermined by the client's brief.

Consider the content

When making these choices you need to take into account how the illustrations you use will affect the character of the job. For example, whimsical hand-drawn illustration may be appropriate for a book on traditional cookery, but would look out of place in a technical publication, where photographic images would be a more suitable choice. Often the decision on illustrations is closely linked to layout. For some types of job, such as instruction manuals or 'how to' books, you may have to plan for series of step-by-step photographs or illustrations. You will need to think ahead about how these will work on your design grid and how the images will relate to any

captioning that is provided. Detailed decisions that you will also need to make include the range of colours to be used, the weight of line and the form in which the illustrations will be submitted.

Using photography

Although many of the technical considerations relating to photography remain in the realm of the photographer, as a graphic designer using photographic images in your work, there are aspects of the craft of photography that you need to understand to make the most of the images you commission and use.

In many cases where specific photographic images are required – for example, to illustrate factual information such as instructional text, the graphic designer is also required to direct the photographer to obtain the images that are demanded by the brief. You may be involved in tasks as varied as selecting models, choosing props and arranging sets. You may also be working closely with the photographer on composing the shots to fit layouts. In some cases you will be supported by others with specific skills such as food stylists.

Working with film

One of the main considerations is what format film is appropriate for the job in hand. The size at which the images are to be used is fundamental. For every picture taken there is an enlargement ratio. In cinema this is 30,000 per cent – the

*As an art director on a shoot you have commissioned, you will be involved in the **choice of model** and the 'look' required to meet the requirements of your design.*

picture quality is degraded by massive enlargement, but this goes largely unnoticed because of the distance of the viewer from the screen. The tolerable enlargement ratio for the printed page is much less: for a transparency it is 100–1,500 per cent. At 900 per cent enlargement, a 35mm image would cover a whole magazine page; for a 5 x 4 inch (125 x 100mm) transparency to cover the same size page the necessary enlargement is only 225 per cent; and an 8 x 10 inch requires only 110 per cent enlargement. As grain is constant regardless of size, the larger formats provide the sharpest images for large-scale work.

Digital photography

As digital cameras are able to take images of increasing quality, more and more photographers are offering this choice of photographic medium. While it is still true that film offers the best quality image, especially for high-quality large format printed applications, for many purposes, notably web design, the difference is academic. Not dissimilar in look to a conventional camera, a digital camera captures its image as data through sensors. This information can then be downloaded from the camera's memory into a personal computer, which is extremely convenient for the graphic designer. There is no cost for film and processing, developing times are non-existent and no scanning is required. Picture resolution needs to be carefully calculated to the size of the image required. In rough terms, a 3.5 million megapixel camera can take a 300dpi shot at A5 size and a 6–7 million megapixel camera can take a A4 shot at that resolution.

Using illustration

Modern reproduction techniques mean that virtually anything that can be scanned and translated into a digital file – from a traditional pencil drawing to a piece of fabric – can now be incorporated into a layout on a computer. Illustration can be defined as an image that fulfils a set brief. It is usually commissioned by a designer or art director who works on behalf of a client. Typically, samples of the illustrator's work are seen in a source book, visited at a website on the Internet, or discussed in person where a portfolio of work is shown. Working in an agreed style, the illustrator then creates a specific image to suit the client's needs. There are specialized fields of illustration and most illustrators are expert in a particular one. It is worth getting to know a few commercial illustrators so that you can commission the one with the most appropriate style for each job. Commissioning illustration for design often brings a level of individuality and standard of finish to a job that the designer could not otherwise achieve.

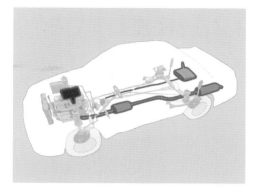

Technical illustration is primarily about conveying information accurately. It may demand the selection and emphasis of certain features, such as the exhaust system in this car illustration, in order to explain the text. The art director must brief the illustrator carefully in order to ensure that the final artwork meets the brief.

Step-by-step photography is one of the mainstays of book illustration. As an all-round graphic designer, you will need to plan and supervise such photography carefully to ensure that everything from the model's clothing to the angle of the shot are right for the job.

Types of photography

Posters, packaging, books, magazines and advertising all rely heavily on photographic images as the anchor around which text is arranged. An artfully cropped picture that conveys the mood may be the key to selling a product, and photographs snapped at the scene of a major news story often provide a valuable sense of immediacy that supports a journalist's report. Both widely different applications of photography have their place.

Photographs in design either form a record of an object or event, or they enhance the concept of the project. Designers have two options when using photography in their work: whether to commission special photography and direct the image required or to source it from existing stock. In all cases, the designer must consider carefully the needs of the graphic project and take into account costs, the limitations of photography and the ability of the photographer to fulfil the brief. The photographer's technical skill in matching your requirements will be a major factor in whether photographic imagery works in the final design. You must also consider copyright and only use images that you have permission to use.

Studio photography

In the studio you have full control over the creation of an image. Through lighting, filtration and the use of special effects, the final result can be fully determined. Extra darkroom manipulation during the developing stage (especially with black-and-white prints), or computer enhancement

*Carefully styled **studio photography** is often the key attraction of best-selling cookery books. A shot such as this usually involves the specialist skills of a home economist, a food stylist and props buyer as well as those of the photographer and art director.*

using an image-manipulation program, will ensure that the desired effect is achieved. Subjects especially suited to studio photography include still life (food and nature) and portraits.

Documentary photography

Photographs taken in natural daylight or with simple flash can capture spontaneous moments and events. Movement, weather change and the rapid transition of events all provide the documentary or reportage photographer with visual texture that lends an immediacy to the images they create and to the projects for which they are then used. Principally attached to newspapers and magazines, photographers working in this specialism are usually briefed for assignments. Advertising campaigns, company reports and sports subjects also often require the skills of a documentary photographer to illustrate themes and concepts that require the 'feel' of reportage.

Image banks

Photographic libraries – dealing in either physical transparencies or increasingly in digital pictures – are an alternative source of images for the graphic designer. There are many image banks operating solely on the Internet. Some images are sold with rights for only a single usage, others are royalty-free and useable forever after the initial charge. You can buy disks of images or download images individually. Investigate this field thoroughly to find which library suits your needs. The biggest players with the most exhaustive libraries are rarely the cheapest, but smaller image banks may be hard to find. A fast Internet connection is invaluable for accessing these resources.

*Set against the quietly constant background of the beach, this piece of **documentary photography** explores the tension between stillness and movement. The eye focuses on the blurring dog as it launches from the side of its resting owner, who sits reflecting in perfect stillness. Such an image could be used successfully in contexts as varied as a magazine article on travel or in a book about health and exercise.*

*Many useful photographs are available from picture libraries. A **simple image**, such as this daisy, could be used in a variety of graphic contexts; for example, on packaging or in an advertisement where its connotations of freshness could be used to good effect. This image was used on a well-known brand of cleansing wipes. The subtle reference to wetness is made by the tiny bead of water resting in the fold of a delicate petal.*

Types of illustration

As a graphic design specialism, illustration has always embraced technology to further its development, from the Chinese woodblock to the vector-based computer drawing program. Whatever means are used to create it, the beauty of the crafted image will always have a place in the business of communication.

Decorative illustration

Illustration is frequently used to embellish textual matter to create visual interest where there may be little other opportunity for the use of images. As in illuminated manuscripts, such decorative illustration may be an embellished capital letter, or even a company logo. Decorative alphabets are a favourite illustrative device. Marginal illustrations and illustrative devices, for example to mark the start and/or end of a chapter, can add character and atmosphere. Other uses for decorative illustration include wrapping paper, textile and fabric design, greetings cards and corporate publications. At times this type of illustration can emphasize form over content and is therefore unsuitable where the illustration needs to explain or enhance the text.

Reportage

Reportage is the illustrative equivalent of photo-journalism. Pictures often drawn and painted on location under pressure have an immediacy and edge that cannot be recaptured in the comfort of the studio. The late Paul Hogarth, Feliks Topolski and Ben Shahn all excelled in this field.

Advertising

Potentially the most lucrative area of work for an illustrator, this genre involves the use of images to sell or support products. As well as appearing in publications and on packaging, advertising images are used on giant billboards, television and in the cinema. Campaigns are often protracted, involving many creative disciplines and teamwork is essential to ensure success. The briefing for the illustrator can be specific and the process can involve numerous revisions.

*Based on a style echoing the spectacular lithographic posters, of Henri de Toulouse Lautrec and Pierre Bonnard, this **colourful melodramatic scene** was the commissioned front cover of a theatre supplement in a national newspaper. The illustrator was asked to recapture the vibrancy of Victorian performance to celebrate a long-established tradition.*

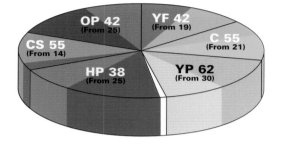

Create **data graphics** such as pie charts and graphs yourself to avoid the generic look of ubiquitous presentation software. This pie chart has been given a three-dimensional look by vertically squashing the graph and adding a bottom section.

This endearing, traditional **children's book illustration** (left) was painstakingly created with mechanical pen, watercolour and gouache.

Books

In works of both fiction and non-fiction, book illustrators think and work with narrative, sequential ideas, linking them to the text content. As visual storytelling, the best pictures are those that add a colour, flavour or hint of meaning but do not try to retell the story for a second time. At the most immediate level, illustrated book jackets need to entice the reader and then hold their interest. Instructional and reference books and manuals are often illustrated throughout, and communication through images and text cannot be separated.

Picture books, teenage fiction, reference and educational works all come within the children's book category. Illustrators may also write the accompanying text. This is a highly specialized branch of illustration that requires well developed skills of imagination. These books need to appeal to both the parents and children, and innovative ideas coupled with appealing imagery are vital. There has recently been a revolution in the illustrated book market and many of the accepted rules of layout and format have been 'bent' or broken by more progressive publishers. This has resulted in some exciting compositional displays of type and image.

Technical illustration

This form of illustration is used to convey highly accurate and specific information. Whatever medium is employed, painstaking attention to detail takes precedence over artistic interpretation. Car manuals, and illustrated maps, plans and artist's impressions for architects all require technical illustration. Technical illustration closely ties into the design specialism of information graphics (see pp.70–1).

Time-based media

Sequences of graphic images are used in film, music, animation and websites. Curiously, the starting point for this discipline is the old-fashioned storyboard, where a set of sketches enables a designer or director to plan their way though segments of 'moving' images, known as frames. The appeal and utility of storyboards has much to do with the way they generate visual ideas. When framed drawing was combined with dialogue and thought, the strip cartoon was born. Storyboarding and strip cartoons have much in common, and the storyboard format has influenced the presentation of many types of information graphics, from D-I-Y manuals to electronic games and multimedia presentations.

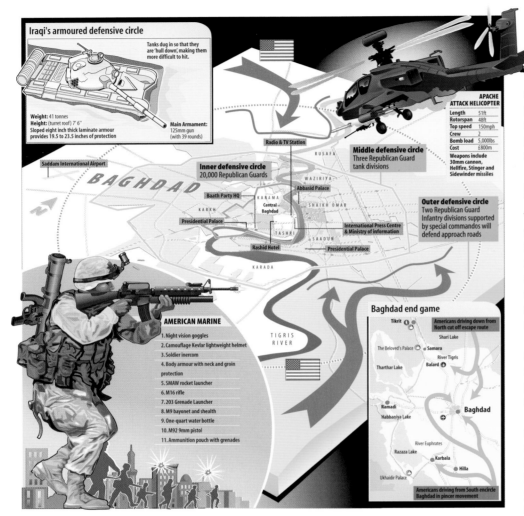

Iraqi's armoured defensive circle

Tanks dug in so that they are 'hull down', making them more difficult to hit.

Weight: 41 tonnes
Height: (turret roof) 7' 6"
Sloped eight inch thick laminate armour provides 19.5 to 23.5 inches of protection

Main Armament: 125mm gun (with 39 rounds)

Saddam International Airport

B A G H D A D

Inner defensive circle
20,000 Republican Guards

Radio & TV Station

RUSAFA

Middle defensive circle
Three Republican Guard tank divisions

APACHE ATTACK HELICOPTER

Length	51ft
Rotorspan	48ft
Top speed	150mph
Crew	2
Bomb load	5,000lbs
Cost	£800m

Weapons include 30mm cannon, Hellfire, Stinger and Sidewinder missiles

WAZIRIYA

Baath Party HQ

Abbasid Palace

KARAMA
Central Baghdad

SHAIKH OMAR

KARKH

Presidential Palace

International Press Centre & Ministry of information

Outer defensive circle
Two Republican Guard Infantry divisions supported by special commandos will defend approach roads

TASHRI

SAADUN

Rashid Hotel

Presidential Palace

KARADA

TIGRIS RIVER

AMERICAN MARINE

1. Night vision goggles
2. Camouflage Kevlar lightweight helmet
3. Soldier inercom
4. Body armour with neck and groin protection
5. SMAW rocket launcher
6. M16 rifle
7. 203 Grenade Launcher
8. M9 bayonet and sheath
9. One-quart water bottle
10. M92 9mm pistol
11. Ammunition pouch with grenades

Baghdad end game

Tikrit

Americans driving down from North cut off escape route

Shari Lake

The Beloved's Palace — Samara

River Tigris

Tharthar Lake — Balard

Ramadi

Baghdad

Habbaniya Lake

River Euphrates

Razaza Lake — Karbala

Hilla

Ukhaidir Palace

Americans driving from South encircle Baghdad in pincer movement

Newspaper graphics

The need to inform the reader using clear, easy-to-follow visuals lies at the heart of the newspaper graphic artist's remit. Images must be colourful enough to enhance the printed page, but not so colourful that they blind the reader with confusing conflicts of tone and hue, preventing other information from being absorbed and distracting from the text.

Information graphics

This graphic design discipline focuses chiefly on the efficient and accurate communication of information, which must be carefully selected, organized and presented. It may require the use of a wide range of visual resources in order to do this, including maps, timetables, graphs, statistical charts, signs, flow diagrams, medical diagrams or cutaway drawings.

Where content is dense, the information designer must also be able to extract what is necessary and decide on the best means of presentation to convey the required message in a graphic format.

The personal computer is now the main tool of the information graphic designer and there are a range of drawing programs that enable the production of clear, colourful, multi-layered images which can be combined with text in a page-layout program. Before the advent of the computer, designers relied on typesetters to produce the type for captions and annotation. These were then cut and pasted by hand onto a line drawing made with technical pens or a tonal image created with dry-letter transfer, or possibly airbrush. Digital technology has speeded the process of graphic work, allowing the modification of elements and easy transmission of the end result to the client.

The function of the larger analysis diagram was to explain and support the news story. Worked to tight deadlines, it is usual for two or more artists to work on such a complex piece of artwork. A sketchy layout was executed and broken down into segments for each member of the team to execute. For this kind of illustration, a researcher is often used to gather source material from photographs, maps and cuttings. The page designer needs to brief the artists on the size and proportion of the graphic, and a leading member of the team should also keep in close contact with the writer of the story, so that accuracy is maintained throughout. Roughs and first proofs are agreed with the editor, and progress is checked at various times of the day. The final proofs are checked by a newspaper sub-editor for accuracy of information and spelling before the final image is placed into the page layout.

Printmaking

Unpredictable and exciting, printmaking offers a variety of attractive options to the graphic designer, especially in the choice of colour, shape, texture and pattern. Printmaking was the first technique used for the reproduction of illustrations in books, magazines and newspapers – first as wood blocks and later in the form of engravings and lithographs.

Artists' ambitions permeated the printer's trade in the nineteenth century and their experimentation with colour and mark-making entered popular visual culture mainly through posters. Although photography and drawn illustration have largely dominated the world of graphic design in the twentieth century, printmaking has much to offer the innovator and combines well with all forms of typography and image-making.

Types of printmaking

Relief printing is the simplest and most common form of printmaking. It involves the removal of material from a block, for example of wood or linoleum, to create a raised image that prints when the surface is covered with ink and pressed onto paper.

Linocut The medium of child's play is raised to the position of high art in this simple process. A design is drawn or traced onto domestic linoleum. Where there is no image or where it is intended as white space, the material is cut away leaving a raised surface. Ink is rolled out over the surface and paper is pressed onto the lino. A stark, solid colour and white print is achieved. With this limited edition book illustration the lino is cut freely and simply as it has no definite grain. The minimal information found in the print is part of the beauty of the process, which is most effective when worked within limitations.

The opposite of relief is 'intaglio' printing. In this method the printing plate is scratched or scored so that the ink sits in the depressions. The surface is wiped clean leaving ink in the grooves. The image is printed onto dampened paper under the pressure of a press. Drypoint (in which the image is scratched into a metal plate) and etching (in which the image is scratched into a wax-covered metal plate, which is then etched in acid) are examples of intaglio printing.

A third group of printing methods are those involving the process of making prints from a flat surface and include lithography and screen-printing. Each type of print has it's own graphic qualities that can bring a special character to a piece of design work. Understanding the different print-making options is not only important from a graphic perspective – offering different possibilities for design – but instils a basic understanding of print reproduction processes.

Working with images

Sometimes the images you are supplied with just don't do the job you need. They may be the wrong format, or they may contain extraneous or distracting elements or faults. With your page layout program and image manipulation software you have the option of adapting the original image to meet the requirements of your design. However, you need to develop the visual skills to help you assess what needs to be done.

Legal considerations

Images come from many sources: specially commissioned from the photographer or illustrator, supplied as transparencies or prints from a picture library, downloaded from a web-based image bank, or supplied by a writer or contributor along with text. Unless you are working with a picture researcher who can be relied on to have dealt with these matters, you need to establish that you have the permission of the copyright holder before using any image – whether photographic or graphic.

Copyright is a very complex area and it is advisable to attend a short course or at least buy a reference book on this subject. In general, you need to make sure that explicit permission has been granted for use of the image in the specific context of the present job and in the markets in which your design work will eventually appear, and that you have paid an agreed fee. Permission may also entail an agreement to credit the source of an image in a particular way. You cannot reuse an image used in a previous job in a new job unless a new permission has been granted. This also applies to commissioned artwork and to photography, unless your agreement with the artist or photographer assigns copyright of the image to you. When images are provided by a contributor you should make sure that they are entitled to give permission for the images to be used. Many authors have collections of photographs in their area of expertise for research purposes, but may not own copyright.

Quality control

Before using a photograph in any professional job, you need to satisfy yourself that it is technically of adequate quality. If you are using a transparency, as soon as you receive it check it carefully with an eye-glass (or loupe) over a light box. Look out for scratches or blemishes that might appear in the printed image. If you find a fault, immediately notify the source, otherwise you could be deemed responsible for the damage. In some cases small faults can be corrected after scanning using an image manipulation program.

You should also check that the image (whether on transparency or a digital image) is in focus and not 'soft' – unless that is an effect you are deliberately seeking.

Apart from technical considerations, when faced with a batch of images, for example, from a

*You will need a **lightbox and loupe** for checking the quality and content of transparencies.*

studio shoot, you will need to use careful judgement when you make your selections. An eye for detail is essential. Look out for small differences between similar shots – for example, an ugly crease in the model's clothing, or someone making an unfortunate expression, or a distracting element in the background. Sometimes details that are easily overlooked in life are jarring in a photo.

Using the image

When you have an image composed in the frame by the photographer, it is important to not to feel restricted by that composition. With the exception of 'art' photographs that should not be altered, photographic images in most graphic design contexts should be viewed as a raw material that can be edited and cropped to suit your purposes.

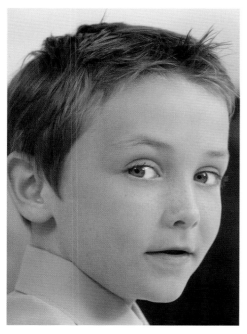

Cropping The most straightforward way of adapting an image to suit your needs is to crop it. This may be simply a matter of altering the proportions of the image to fit the allocated space in your layout. However, you can also use cropping to remove extraneous elements so that the focus is on the main subject or to create a more striking composition. The impact of the original images of the boy (top left) and the leopard (right) is altered according to way in which they are cropped, producing greater intensity when cropped in close.

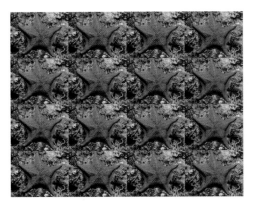

Cut outs *For some types of job, you may wish to remove the background of a photograph so that the main subject is 'cut out' against the background of the page. This allows you to avoid the monotony of squared up pictures and enables you to flow text around an image to create interesting shapes and a more 'organic' composition. Cut outs are widely used in all areas of graphic design and are easily created in a page layout program.*

A single photograph can be repeated – or tiled – to form a **composite image.** *Such an image can be used effectively as a background on a piece of packaging design, for example. Where the image has strong colours and contrasts, as here, it would need to be 'knocked back' in areas where type is needed.*

Vignettes *A vignette is when the background of an image is gradually faded so that it blends into the page. In effect you create a softer type of cut out. The advantage is that the outer part of the image is not lost entirely, providing visual interest in the background, but is progressively knocked back so that type can be overprinted. You can specify the extent of the vignette to suit your needs.*

A photographic image can be used successfully as an interesting textured background for text. **Knocking back** the image in a panel under the area in which the type is to lie ensures readability and can provide an extra design element in your scheme.

Colour manipulation and special effects Programs such as Photoshop allow you to play with the colour balance of an image to create the precise effect you want. This may be a matter of correcting a problem in the original shot to reflect a 'truer' colour, or you may want to achieve particular colour characteristics to meet your design concept. Many different options are available to you, from duotones, to posterization, solarization and sepia-toned effects. It is worthwhile spending time familiarizing yourself with these options and looking out for ways of using them effectively.

TIP

A word of warning: don't become so enamoured of special photographic effects that you use them without good reason in your designs. They should work with your overall design concepts rather than dominating them.

Stylization in illustration

Stylization of drawing is a method commonly employed by illustrators to give visual information a particular emphasis and style, often obscuring somewhat the object or setting, while leaving it still recognizable. In this project, the technique was chosen to create a visual identity for a conference that was held in Philadelphia, USA. A new image was needed to convey the intended information to the delegates.

The brief

The building chosen as the key image for this project was Independence Hall, Philadelphia, USA, the location of the signing of the US Constitution, and an international symbol of freedom. The artist was commissioned to produce the illustration because his spontaneous and direct style and love of architectural rendering were most suited to the initial ideas suggested by the client. The approach to the job was slightly unusual as the client was not entirely sure exactly what kind of image they wanted. It was a classic case of 'knowing what we want when we see it'. This element of exploration made the job all the more enjoyable. The message was that the image needed to be instantly recognizable to delegates visiting the city. The image needed to be authoritative, welcoming and majestic, but spontaneously drawn, carrying the spirit of an observational sketchbook visit, accurately drawn but not too detailed so as to be usable at a variety of sizes.

Media and first thoughts

A combination of fine-liner and Japanese brush was chosen for the job. These tools produced spontaneous marks that create fresh and above all simple images. By altering the pressure he applied to the brush, the illustrator was able to give the drawings considerable 'weighting' and a sense of firmness and solidity. The illustrator was not able to visit the city but used the Internet to find visual references for his initial roughs, before gaining quality photographs from an image stock library.

*The **original drawing** was a straight rendering of the building from secondary sources.*

*The artist simplified the symmetrically ordered façade and reduced it to a limited collection of **lines and shapes**. Some areas, such as the windows and tower arches, were filled with black ink. A small shadow running down the inside edge of the tower helped to create a three-dimensional effect.*

*As the drawings progressed, the information was reduced, and the constant question for the artist was 'how far can I keep **stripping away the detail** before the building ceases to be recognizable?'*

*The artist developed a kind of **shorthand drawing notation**, using collective groupings of flecks and dashes and sweeps of the brush to denote architectural detail. Arches became mere loops and colonnades, short-pressured strokes.*

*The designer chose this image, which seemed best to balance the qualities of **expressiveness and clarity**.*

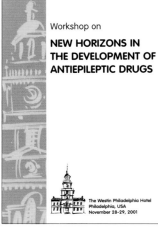

Workshop on

NEW HORIZONS IN THE DEVELOPMENT OF ANTIEPILEPTIC DRUGS

The Westin Philadelphia Hotel
Philadelphia, USA
November 28–29, 2001

*The **final image** was used in three different colours at three different sizes, so that at no time was there incorrect balance or visual conflict. By making wide use of white space, the designer allowed the images to communicate fully in their context.*

Including images on the design grid

An engaging design requires a considered balance of text and image even when the pictorial element is actually typographic in nature. Whatever the constraints of your source material, be it copy heavy or image rich, there is usually some space to play around with for contrast and balance. A flexible typographic scheme can usually be adapted to be sympathetic to the supporting imagery without defying the internal logic of the page design.

Images at work

The following pages contain a series of examples of photographs in a graphic design context. In some cases they dominate the design, in others the image plays a supporting role to the text. It is a useful exercise to note in each case how the designer has visually balanced the text and illustration areas to provide a pleasing composition of elements on the page.

Using the grid

Adherence to the discipline of a well-thought out design grid makes the task of planning images into your layouts easier. It is also important to rememember that white space on the page – whether as areas without image or type or as areas of generous leading between lines of type – is one of your design elements; it should be actively included in your creative planning.

Careful consideration should also be given to other aspects of how you use the images, such as whether they should bleed off the page margin or sit within the grid. You will need to consider whether you want to frame each image in box rule and if so of what weight.

In this layout from a **cookery book**, the photograph occupying the whole of the left-hand page carries equal weight with the text. It has been cropped to provide a close-up that communicates the texture of the cream.

*Documentary-style black-and-white photography has been used to good effect in this layout. The juxtaposition of **images of different sizes** and the bold typography combine to create an energetic yet ordered effect.*

Rome: open-neck city. It's that Italian style thing. Soft-shouldered jackets, sports shirts, dark glasses at noon. For the first in our regular fashion series, Scottish photographer David Eustace flew south, hung around the streets of the eternal city and took pictures of men who showed an innate sense of style. 'Fortunately, I had a young, female Italian assistant,' he says. 'She's the one who asked these guys if I could photograph them. I'm glad I didn't have to do the approaching.'

Main picture Jacket:
Ermenegildo Zegna £375
Polo shirt: Tread by
Carrefaini £100
Sunglasses: web £120
Watch: Baume
& Mercier £1650

Below Blazer: Ralph
Lauren Polo £375
Shirt: Biffi, Milan £120
Trousers: Dockers £40

ON THE CORNER:
ROMANTICISM

*The **cover image** of this directory does not need to convey information – it is used solely to create a mood. The silhouette of the figure provides a bold graphic shape that complements the typography. The knocked-back images on the inside pages continue the theme of the cover and help to 'lift' what would otherwise be visually tedious text-only pages.*

SIBECASIA2004

directory

A Business Forum for the
Health, Fitness & Spa Industry
26-28 February 2004
The Shangri La Tanjung Aru Resort, Kota Kinabalu, Malaysia

SIBECASIA2004

》 **Algotherm/Groupe BATTEUR Hong Kong**
Delegate: Kilroy Wassir, Export Area Manager

Flat D, 6/F
World Trust Tower
50 Stanley Street
Central
Hong Kong

Tel: +812 234 5674
Fax: +812 234 5674
Email: kilroywassir@algotherm.com
Web: www.algotherm.com.hk

Product Category: Cosmetics

Profile:

The Algotherm Marine Cosmetics Laboratory was created in the 1960's by a very talented scientist who had a passion for the sea and who pioneered the use of seaweed in cosmetology. The production site is situated in a privileged part of Brittany where 80% of the seaweed used in cosmetology are harvested.

Algotherm has devoted all its professional competence in the development of pure, effective and rigorously tested products. With this aim and in order to optimise the treatments and ensure the best results, Algotherm has perfected an exclusive and innovative protocol for the use of its skin and body care products. This methodology for beauty and well-being called 'The Methodology of the 5 Senses' has been developed and validated by the Algotherm team of experts. This original concept has been adopted by beauticians in salons and Thalassotherapy centers to ensure that every Algotherm treatment is a moment of well-being and pleasure.

Algotherm beauty therapists are experts in skin care and body care who are trained to perform the specific treatments in our international school located in the Algotherm Thalassotherapy Center in Deauville.

44   d i r e c t o r y

SIBECASIA2004

》 **Babor Cosmetics Asia-Pacific Ltd**
Delegate: John Donne, Sales & General Director

Neuenhofstr 123
Aachen 12345
Germany

Mobile: +49 123 456 7890
Email: john.donne@babor.de
Web: www.babor.de

Product Category: Cosmetics

Profile:

BABOR is an internationally orientated family owned company located in Aachen, Germany. With more than 50 years experience in the Skin Care Business, BABOR today is the market leader in Germany and one of the most important European cosmetic companies in the professional distribution channel. The company's aim is the development, production and distribution of cosmetic products within a selective distribution channel, mainly in Cosmetic Institutes, high-class Hotels, selective Parfumeries, International Department Stores, Spas and Duty Free Shops. BABOR offers a wide range of high-quality skin and body care products based on as far as possible natural ingredients, always focussing on the latest scientific standard, as well as several other product series such as Make-up, Sun Care, Whitening, etc. All processes are based on a Total Quality Management. With the high production standards, BABOR is even allowed under the severe EU regulations to produce pharmaceuticals – proof of the highest quality of our products and the production standards. Intensive in-house research and close co-operation with universities guarantee solid scientific expertise, extremely high product quality, stability as well as continual outstanding product innovations, setting exacting standards which are also reflected in its rigorous training programs. Welcome to the World of Babor: "The most beautiful me"

d i r e c t o r y   45

Maintaining design consistency

On these pages there are three very different but congruent double-page spreads from a book on hippy culture. All three spreads clearly belong to the same work, despite being so varied, because an underlying visual scheme is in place for both image and text. Where possible, images dominate the right-hand page (recto) while text occupies the left-hand page (verso). The verso page is tonally more dense in its top half. The typographic design is classic – a sans serif typeface with a full range of weights is used – and the hierarchy of information headings and types is clearly defined. Body copy sits on generous leading for legibility and in three justified columns for maximum density, creating space for display. Image and text have been given room to breathe separately in this design and do not directly interfere with each other. Harmony is achieved by setting the text in the same tonal range and visual feel of the imagery it accompanies.

*This **section opener** uses bold condensed display type reversed out of a solid background to provide strong contrasts. This graphically powerful device helps the reader to find each section easily, while subconsciously registering the style common to title pages.*

An appropriate image has been found and sized to counterbalance the typography. Sumptuous curves echo those of the large year display typeface and the hard tonal contrast of the picture resonates well with the text page.

*In this spread there is a **satisfying alignment** of both cap line and baseline from the quotation on the left-hand page to the word 'whisky' within the image on the right-hand page, anchoring our attention. The body text, set in two columns, leaves white space for the absent third column, echoing a similar negative space in the image on the facing page. The line spacing of the body text fortuitously resembles the strokes in the circle and skirt in the picture and, although this particular effect may be a happy accident, the sizing and cropping choices for the image will have played a part in exploiting this potential. The left-hand page when taken in isolation is simply a piece of clean yet unexceptional typography. However, when viewing the spread as a whole as intended, we see that elements of equal density have been arranged in compositional harmony, creating a rewarding design.*

d'imposteurs, et encore des sorciers, des enchanteurs et des magiciens. Les dissidents des Rose-Croix aux guetteurs d'OVNI en passant par la secte sataniste de Crowley, aucune période de l'histoire n'aura jamais produit, en si peu de temps, une telle quantité de théories et de croyances délirantes.

LE RÉVEIL DES EXCLUS

L'heure où les Noirs vont enfin cesser d'être les grands exclus de la société américaine approche. En ce sens, les « années hippies » coïncident avec la radicalisation d'un combat qui s'annonce long, âpre et sanglant. Les années 1960 ne sont pas seulement dominées par la personnalité de Martin Luther King, devenu l'homme à abattre dès qu'il s'oppose à la guerre du Vietnam. C'est également le temps de la révolte des Black Panthers. Après avoir assisté, impuissants, aux massacres de leurs frères par les forces de l'ordre, ils prennent les armes en 1967 et ripostent. Les chiffres, terribles, parlent d'eux-mêmes : les émeutes font quatre-vingt-trois morts, dont vingt-trois à Newark et quarante-trois à Detroit, et plusieurs milliers de blessés. Detroit brûle en juillet de cette année. Des tireurs d'élite sont perchés sur les toits, et quatre mille sept cents parachutistes de l'US Army, épaulés par huit mille soldats de la garde nationale, sont mobilisés pour occuper le ghetto en

flammes. Rien d'étonnant à ce que les Black Panthers soient armés : l'assassinat de Martin Luther King prouve l'inanité d'une protestation pacifique face à un pouvoir raciste. Le massacre des Noirs par la police, qui tire pour tuer, se déroule pendant que les hippies, issus de la classe moyenne, passent l'été sous le signe de l'amour. Une situation qu'il convient de ne pas perdre de vue.

Aux États-Unis, les années 1960 auront été cruciales pour l'évolution du statut des Noirs – comme pour celui des femmes. Si aujourd'hui, nul ne s'étonne plus de les trouver à tous les échelons de la société, de l'armée jusqu'au secteur des affaires, il y a trente ans, la chose était impensable, voire choquante dans l'esprit de beaucoup de gens.

À GAUCHE TOUTE !

L'orientation politique du mouvement *underground* se cristallise à la fin des années 1960, quand il s'assume de gauche. Selon les mots de David Widgery, la contre-culture conjugue « le bolchevisme dans sa dimension libertaire avec le marxisme dans sa forme la plus généreuse et la plus pertinente ». Jerry Rubin épouse cette même ligne politique, tout comme Ed Sanders, Wavy Gravy et d'autres chefs de file de ce mouvement. Pour cause d'ego surdimensionnés, la théorie connaîtra évidemment des entorses… Si le

mouvement *underground* est globalement marqué à gauche, il incline plutôt vers l'anarchisme. En cela, il ne peut être confondu avec un quelconque parti marxiste ou socialiste. Il n'en joue pas moins un rôle politique important, tant aux États-Unis qu'en Grande-Bretagne. Les hippies remettent en question le sacro-saint respect de l'ordre établi. Leur action contestataire conduit l'ensemble de la société à exiger, de la part des institutions et des politiques, plus de transparence et un comportement plus responsable. En Grande-Bretagne, le mouvement hippie ébranle profondément une hiérarchie sociale étouffante et rigide, même si le système survit à sa remise en question et perdure encore.

L'ensemble de ces pans de liberté arrachés ne peut, bien sûr, être attribué à la seule action du mouvement hippie. Cependant, la remise en question du système aura eu pour effet de sensibiliser l'opinion. Une lame de fond, portée par les peuples, pointera les carences d'une société percluse d'archaïsmes et d'égoïsmes. En réclamant l'octroi de droits et la prise en compte d'exigences trop longtemps refusées, elle emportera bien des rigidités et bien des scléroses.

CI-DESSUS ET À DROITE : Les pochettes d'album sont le terrain privilégié de toutes les surenchères novatrices. Elles seront finalement reconnues comme un art à part entière.
PAGES 24-25 : *Easy Rider*, 1969.

22

*Whereas the section openers in this book used one large picture and bold typography, the **end of a chapter** allows for a more playful approach. The image extends into the top half of the left-hand page. The text has been left plenty of room to breathe. The images bleed off the page, letting the eye wander pleasurably after completing the text, promoting a sense of reflection and completion.*

TIP

Half squint at the example spreads to see them in terms of contrast and tone; observe how well image and text harmonize. When conceiving layouts, make quick initial thumbnail sketches to 'block in' the light and dark areas until you find a balance. These thumbnails will be invaluable at layout stage.

Working to a brief

Graphic design is primarily a service industry; your aesthetic preferences are important but secondary to the successful fulfilment of a brief to the client's ultimate satisfaction. By cultivating good communication and negotiation skills you will reduce the likelihood of feeling compromised. Placing the clients needs first while protecting your own interests will ensure that you retain clients and gain new ones through recommendation.

Initial considerations

During your earliest discussions with a client about a job you need to ascertain certain basic parameters for the brief. These include the design budget, the job specification, the print run, the deadline and/or schedule and exactly what the client is intending to communicate in the finished product. Find out where the job is being printed and who is handling this aspect of the job. It is also important to obtain contact details for everyone involved with the brief. Discuss where responsibility for various aspects of the job lies – for example, who is responsible for supplying images and from where. After this initial meeting pause to take stock of the situation before providing a written quotation and proposing a detailed schedule.

The fee and contract

Talk about money as early in the process as you can and do not commence any major works without agreement on your fee, preferably by the client's signature on a contract. When you first start out, financial negotiation can be daunting so it may help to build your pricing structure around a rough hourly rate. Take an educated guess at how long a job may take, add 20 per cent (for administration and overruns) and then consider what a plumber, electrician or carpenter might charge for the equivalent time. The amount of the total budget for design and layout, images, illustration, print, finishing and delivery will affect both the technical limits of a job and the amount of concept time that you can afford to devote to it. The more elements of a budget that you handle personally, the more flexibility you will have. It is common practice for the designer to source print quotations and handle the dealings with the printer themselves – a reasonable charge for print handling is around 10 per cent of the total print cost. If a client wants to source their own print then you just supply the files and take no further responsibility for the proofing and printing schedule.

It helps to talk about any copyright issues as soon as possible. It is quite usual to send some form of contract and/or terms and conditions for approval. For large jobs, clients may send terms of their own; read them carefully seeking legal advice if necessary. If you are not happy with part of the contract, then renegotiate. You should ask for a simple faxed or emailed approval to proceed at any stage of a job. Building this level of paper-work into the process can save you serious problems later on.

From design to print

Get your concept work right. There is no point embarking on a lengthy dead end, so early quick thumbnail sketches sent back and forth rapidly will save a lot of time. In general, it is a good idea to communicate frequently and honestly with your client throughout the brief. Give your client the best first proofs that the budget will allow and explain that they are not totally colour accurate and refer them to printed samples, if necessary. It is sensible to spellcheck a document before proofing, but it is the client's ultimate responsibility to proof-read a job and return a marked-up hard copy for correction. For all but the largest jobs, expect two proofing stages plus some final tweaking. Beyond this it is reasonable to charge an additional fee.

Once you have received a written sign-off from the client to go to print and you have checked the separations and colours to your own satisfaction then you can send the job to print. It is important to understand that things can and do go wrong with print. A bad print error may force the whole job to be rerun and who pays for this depends on where the liability rests. You can refer certain errors (such as typos) back to the client. Similarly, if the print does not match your separations and proof then the error is with the printer. Everything else is down to the designer and will come out of your own pocket. Nobody likes to see a job go wrong so try to catch as many errors as you can throughout the process.

TIP

Remember to request at least three copies of the finished publication or product for your files as part of your fee. This can be easy to forget and it is more awkward to ask for this after a job has been completed.

CHECKLIST

Initial briefing_____

Job description_____

Print specification_____

Print run_____

Design budget

Print budget_____

Print quotations and choice of printer_____

Copyright issues_____

Images, photography, illustration_____

Deadline_____

Responsibilities

Client supplies *(i.e. flatplan, copy, images, etc)*

I supply *(i.e. layout, print handling, scanning, etc)*_____

Quotation_____

Job approval form ☐ sent

Terms and conditions ☐ sent ☐ agreed

Schedule ☐ sent ☐ signed and returned

☐ proposed ☐ signed and returned

Design schedule ☐ agreed

Initial concepts

Thumbnails sent ☐ discussed

First proofs sent ☐ returned ☐ approved

Second proofs sent ☐ returned ☐ amended

Third proofs sent ☐ returned ☐ amended

Approved for print ☐ returned ☐ amended

Job confirmation form sent ☐ ☐ amended

☐ returned

Printing Schedule ☐ amended

Book print and agree schedule

Check separations

Send collected files with inkjet or laser proofs ☐

Check printers proof ☐

Go ahead with print ☐

Check print schedule in progress ☐

☐

☐

☐

Print delivery

Delivery confirmed

Client approved ☐

Send invoice ☐

☐

Working in relief

Working in physical layers that gradually build out from a flat surface allows the designer to create the most dynamic and effective pieces of visual communication. The combination of surfaces of different heights – especially where colour or texture offers strong contrasts – adds extra interest to the design process and gives greater scope to designers' creativity. This abstract relief uses simple colours and shapes, working together in a layered image. The exercise opens up possibilities for the application of relief techniques to practical projects such as packaging.

1 First consider your aims for the piece and its intended message. You may wish to make simple shape and colour sketches along with noted ideas to assist the early stages. In this example, a range of strong, flat colours of equal tonal weighting were selected. The 220gsm card was light enough to be easily cut, yet durable enough to be folded and manipulated.

2 The choice of carefully cut, strong geometric and abstract shapes (squares, long rectangular strips, triangles and a coil) was a direct result of research into the work of others. Contrasts such as static versus movement, long versus short, large versus small were considered to assist the effective layering of a relief image.

3 The blue base was deliberately set at an angle to break the conventional position of a square on the printed page. The slightly smaller square of yellow laid on the base allows the blue to show through. Contrasts were created through the positioning of small, randomly cut squares around a large, centred, cut rectangle. The cut-out pieces were raised and secured by small adhesive pads cut to size and placed beneath the card.

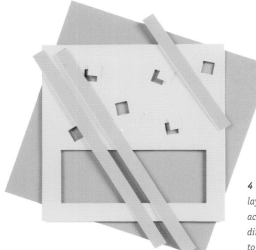

4 *Further contrasts were provided by a third layer of green card strips placed diagonally across the composition. Although strong, this directional movement does not dominate due to the thinness of the strips.*

5 *Helping to balance and unify the created tensions existing within the composition, a tight, red coil was positioned onto the intersection point of all the layers. In addition to the physical layer occupied by the coil, a strong illusion of space was established by the use of complementary colours – red over green – and a succession of shadows back through to the blue base.*

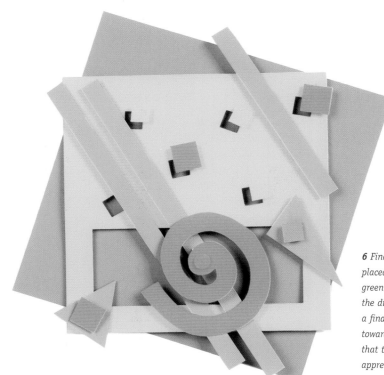

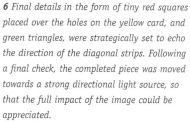

6 *Final details in the form of tiny red squares placed over the holes on the yellow card, and green triangles, were strategically set to echo the direction of the diagonal strips. Following a final check, the completed piece was moved towards a strong directional light source, so that the full impact of the image could be appreciated.*

Cutting and folding techniques

Quality of craftsmanship is of paramount importance in graphic design. It is an indicator of the value of the item or product and a well-made package or three-dimensional construction is immediately attractive. Basic cutting and folding (paper engineering) skills are of practical value and can also enhance the aesthetic of your work. Once learned, they will be part of your stock-in-trade, and problem-solving in three-dimensions will be far easier.

TIP

Always use a sharp blade. Blunted or broken ones require more applied pressure to make a cut, which can increase the risk of your hand slipping. The newer the blade, the cleaner the cut.

EXERCISES

Successful paper modelling, especially through folding, has simplicity and beauty – achieved through clean lines – and precision, which directly affects its success or failure as a functional construction. A mastery of basic paper engineering provides an excellent link into interior design, 3-D design or product design.

You will need a sharp, craft knife or scalpel and a safe surface on which to cut. This should preferably be a purpose-made plastic cutting mat, although a thick piece of cardboard will suffice. This protective layer will protect your work surface and will also stop your work from slipping around.

Paper can be manipulated and shaped without ever having to cut it. By simple bending and folding, it can be raised out of two-dimensional flatness and given the status of low relief. More sophisticated techniques can transform the paper into shapes such as cones or tubes. Any smooth, sized or coated paper or thin card can be used for folding. Thick card lacks the necessary flexibility and will split when scored. Conversely, soft papers and tissues will not fold into a definite crease.

Scoring *Where a clean, sharp fold is required, score the paper halfway through so that it will bend along the scored line. The pressure applied to the knife is critical. Too much and you could cut through, too little and you won't achieve a clean fold. For straight lines, score along a metal rule. If you require a less sharp crease, instead of a knife, use an old ballpoint pen, which acts as a blunter blade.*

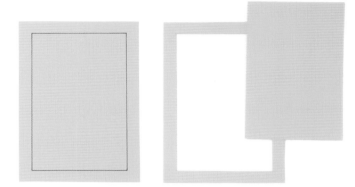

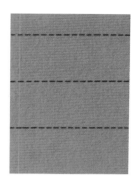

Clean cutting *Rule up the area to be cut and mark it with a pen or pencil line, as shown. Lay a safety rule along the line and apply pressure onto the rule with your non-cutting hand. Hold the craft knife firmly and cut through the line in the direction of the outside of the box and away from your supporting hand. This technique is known as 'cutting to waste' and should be used at all times to prevent accidents and mistakes. Cut only as far as the line. When you have cut all four edges, remove the central rectangle.*

Concertina folding *By raising surfaces, you allow light to reflect off them, thus creating areas of light and shadow. One of the simplest, most effective techniques is the concertina fold. Draw dotted lines across a wide strip of paper at intervals of about 2cm (³/₄in). Score the lines and then turn over the paper and draw and score further lines across the reverse side between the original scored lines. Finally, fold the paper back and forth into a series of reversed creases. The sharp changes in direction break the surface into a pattern of light and dark.*

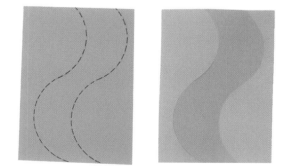

Cutting curves *Cutting in a curve requires your full concentration with a firm but gentle pressure directed towards the tip of the knife blade. As you begin cutting, turn the paper beneath so that the blade cuts in the direction of your turn. Try to keep the paper on the move and your incisions as broad sweeps of the blade. If the shape you are removing is not needed in your design work, then you can cut out to the edge from the centre.*

Curves *cannot be folded without first being scored. Once scored, the paper can be 'lifted' into three-dimensions. To raise the shape as shown in the serpentine curve on blue paper, two equidistant curves need to be drawn (shown here as a dotted line). Score one line on one side of the paper and repeat on the opposite side for the second line. Gently bend the paper in opposing directions and an elegant, sloping channel will run through it.*

Pop-up card

Pop-up products are an exciting area of paper engineering for the graphic designer. Commonly seen in greetings cards and children's books, at their simplest, pop-ups are based upon simple scoring and folding, and at their most sophisticated, they are driven by complex mechanisms containing card, levers and cogs. You can obtain books that contain in-depth information on pop-up techniques with patterns and construction notes.

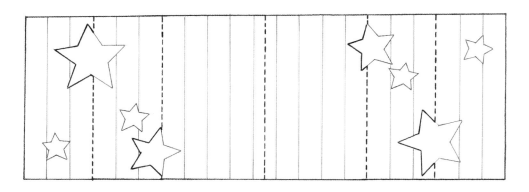

1 Mark up your card with dotted lines and star shapes as indicated in the suggested pattern. Note that the two central panels are slightly larger than the end panels.

2 Decorate the surfaces with your own designs and colours using a bold flat medium such as watercolour (used here), gouache or acrylic. Score gently along the dotted lines and cut only the sections of the stars indicated by the bold lines. Fold the card back and forth along the scored lines and gently lift the cut edges.

3 Draw the clown by copying this template, paying particular attention to the placement of the dotted lines that will need to be folded. The size of the clown is important; the top of his hat should just protrude over the top of the card. Colour him in bright, flat hues.

*4 **Fold along the dotted lines** to obtain sharp creases. Carefully cut around the outline of the clown with a scalpel, and then fix him with a couple of dabs of PVA glue on either side of the central fold of the two larger panels on the concertina folded card. Do not glue over the whole surface of the clown or he will not 'pop-up'.*

*5 **Fold the card** up into its concertina when the glue is dry, and place in a matching envelope.*

TIP:

Consider the size of the card, bearing in mind that it may need to fit a standard envelope. If it is of an unusual size, you will need to make your own.

Creating 3-D packages

Simplicity and good structure, including exact measuring, fine-cutting and clean construction, are the keys to successful packaging. Care and patience on the part of the designer are essential. The best way to learn about what makes a good package is to construct a few yourself.

EXERCISE

Start with the pattern technically known as a 'net'. Decide on the size that most comfortably suits your needs (remembering that a larger container will require a heavier weight of card or paper) and photocopy the net, scaling up or down accordingly. There are non-copyright books available containing variations of bags and boxes or you can carefully dismantle an existing bag or box and use it as the pattern from which to make a template. A lightbox is very useful for this, as it will allow you to make accurate copies onto your chosen paper, by tracing the outlines through the illuminated original beneath. The dotted lines indicate where scoring and folding is necessary.

For this project a smooth-grain, 90gsm parchment paper was purchased from a specialist paper retailer. Extra decoration was incorporated through a simple cut-out pattern of stripes and triangles. Metallic blue paper was stuck behind the cut-out area. This was cut out on the patterns for box and bag before either had been constructed

Making a maquette

Always make a dummy or 'maquette' box or bag first to ensure that it will work. For this purpose, use thin card or cartridge paper. When you are satisfied that the prototype is functional and accurate, proceed to make the final piece.

Choosing materials

The simpler and less complicated your raw materials the better, as this will allow you to focus on the most important part of the process – the accurate making of the package. Too often, over-fussy solutions to a design brief cloud the inherent beauty present in the elementary and straightforward answer. Employing the plainest papers and taking an honest approach will keep you focused on the task in hand and greatly enhance your chances of success.

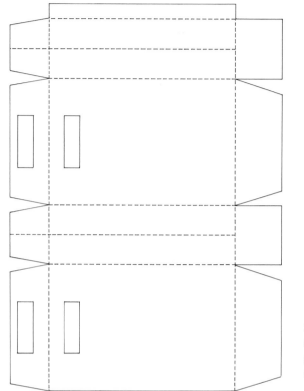

*These nets are for the paper **carrier bag and rectangular gift box** that are shown on the facing page.*

TIP:

Keep any drawn outlines, keylines or guidelines as light as possible, by using a well-sharpened HB pencil. These can be easily erased after the net has been cut out.

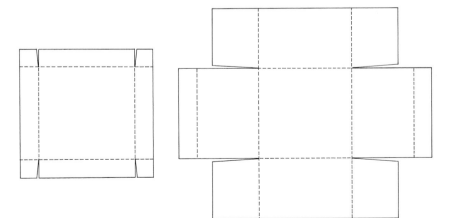

Product packaging

A brand must be instantly recognizable and attractive to the potential customer. This can be achieved only after much consideration and research and by careful packaging that successfully combines typefaces, logos, colours and composition. If the market researchers and designers have not done their work properly, the product may not sell.

The subject for this packaging exercise is a fictitious brand of upmarket Japanese saki, called 'Jitsumi'. The project involves a combination of accurate net drawing and cutting, thumbnail sketches and working drawings, hand-drawn images and typesetting. Access to a computer is not essential for this project; accurate, hand-rendered type is quite acceptable for visualizing.

Body copy printed from the computer, or dry-letter transfer, is fine for design roughs and dummy packages. Photocopying, cut and paste, and collage are all well-established hands-on methods. Where the position of smaller type needs to be indicated, horizontal lines convey this information perfectly adequately. It is also good practice in drawing and appreciating typography.

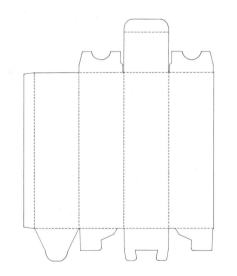

*1 It was decided that the wine would be contained in a standard, clear bottle, and the bottle housed in a presentation box. The **net for the box** was researched from a similar wine-box design. The net was drawn up as shown in the diagram, making sure that the dimensions of the bottle fitted comfortably into the length and width of a side panel.*

*2 Drawings were made to devise **a suitable logo**, which was based on a Japanese character. Colour roughs were rapidly sketched on a layout pad to devise a suitable colour scheme. Upmarket products tend to be simple, with minimal but strong design elements, limited colour and elegant typography. Black and white were chosen for oriental-style simplicity.*

*3 **The display font** was deliberately selected for its understated quality and modern feel. It was felt that it harmonized well with the elegant, linear quality of the logo. Once selected, it was drawn by hand and reversed out using a photocopier to save time. However, if necessary, it could have been hand-rendered too.*

4 *The next set of sketches involved the placing and spacing of* **type on the net and the bottle**. *A critical part of the process, it was important not to 'overcrowd' the available space, but equally there needed to be enough text to contain all the necessary information about the product.*

5 *Once the designs had been finalized, the net template was scanned into the computer and translated to a vector-based program, where the type was set. The scanned logo was imported in a recognized file format. The* **labels for the bottle** *and bottle neck were produced using the same program. It was decided to 'dress' the bottle with a decorative tag. This was a simplified version of the label, displaying only the logo on the outside, and a duplication of relevant box notes on the inside. A small hole was punched in the tag and a straw-coloured rafia tie added the perfect finishing touches.*

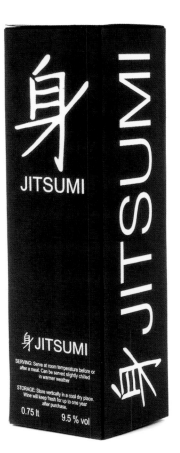

Point-of-sale unit

Weathered pebbles, their wetted blue and green patterns shimmering in the rising sunlight; deeply curving shadows cast by eroded breakwaters, contrasting strongly with the sun-bleached surfaces. A morning spent combing the beach provided a wealth of inspiration from which to devise a point-of-sale unit to sell a range of body products in a typical retail outlet.

With so many product lines vying for counter space, designers must seek to package and display products in a simple and eye-catching way. This project focuses on a point-of-sale unit for a range of men's toiletries entitled 'Marin'. The name carries a sense of the organic freshness of the sea, coupled with the power of the elements, creating two strong themes for this masculine commodity. A sense of calm was to be sustained through the translucent turquoise greens and blues of the liquid gels and soaps. The unit was to be made of lightweight cardboard so that it could be placed on top of a counter. A shower-gel bottle and soap were to be held firmly in position using rebated slots cut into a false card bottom of the box. A backdrop image behind the items was to be designed onto a card panel glued to the back of the box.

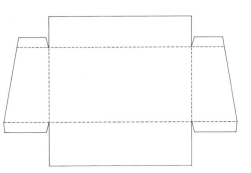

1 Unit construction *Next, the nets were drawn up for the construction of the unit. In this case a simple net for a shallow box was chosen from a book of nets and adjusted to work for this point-of-sale display. A template was made in card using the techniques described on pages 82–3. The images of pebbles on the beach, now converted into a tonal, black-and-white image were fixed to this template.*

Research

A morning photographic shoot on the pebbly shore supplied colour images with strong tones and contrasts. The coloured pebbles made the images look very busy and it was decided that they would be converted to black and white. The images all exhibited natural levels of black, white and grey as a tinted backdrop against the hint of colour splashing into the foreground bottles and packets. It was intended that this would direct full attention to the minimally coloured products.

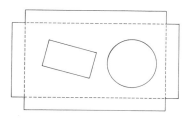

2 The net for the insert false base *was also outlined and the bases of products outlined in the correct position for display. The elements of the unit were carefully cut out and the structure assembled.*

3 An image of sculptural forms *of the weather-worn wooden breakers was selected for the backdrop, as it particularly exemplified the illusion of depth with a full range of tones. This image was dry-mounted with spray adhesive to a sheet of heavy card, and this card in turn was stuck to the back of the box.*

4 Labels *For labelling, simple type in a fresh sea-blue colour was considered the best option for legibility over the textured, photographic images. The natural outer definition of the pebbles gave the labels their shape, and these were printed out, carefully cut and stuck to sample bottles. The swing ticket was designed by using the same pebble shape twice, hinged together to form an irregular-shaped single spread booklet. The inner information was set in blue and black. The front was left as a blank pebble.*

5 The display *Once the engineering had been accurately completed, shredded packing paper, available from craft shops and paper retailers, was laid around the false base to create an attractive 'nest' in which to sit the products.*

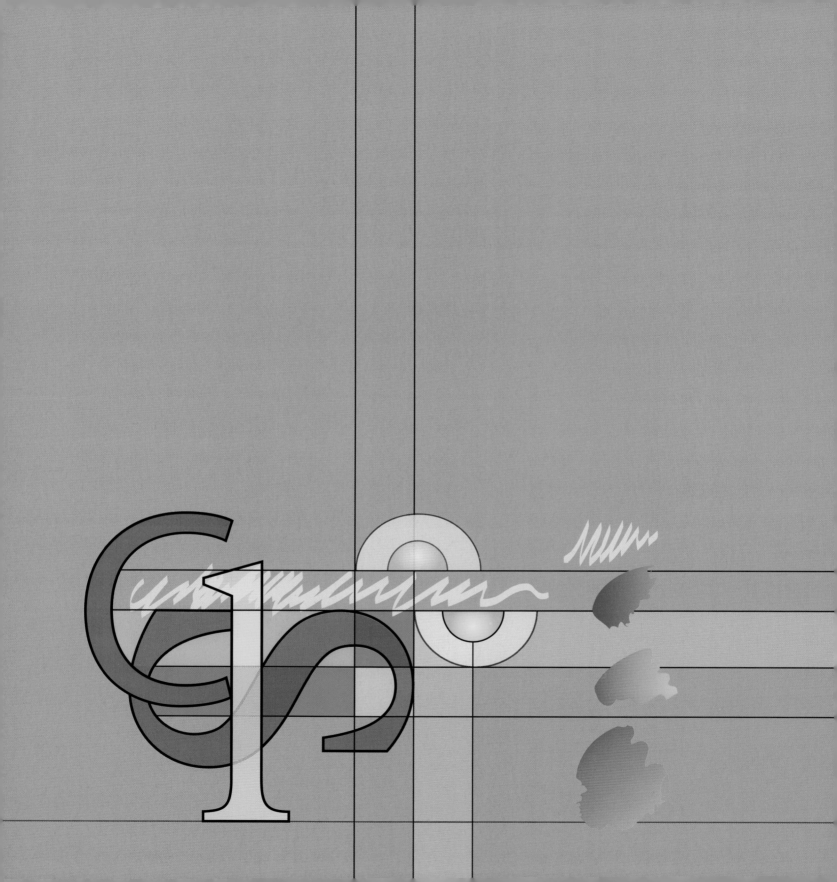

COMPUTERS AND PRODUCTION

Using the computer

The computer is a marvellous invention, but it cannot draw, design or think for you. Although an integral part of the modern design process, a computer is merely a tool to be mastered and used well. Remember that good design still begins with a pencil; allow your concepts, rather than the process, to drive your designs.

First principles

Start by reading the manuals that come with your hardware, they are generally informative and helpful. It is often, however, difficult to elicit software information from the manual that accompanies the package. You will probably find that the best software advice comes from one of the many third-party manuals on the market, some magazines also contain excellent practical tips and tutorials.

Menus and palettes

As you begin to learn how to use your software, you will need to familiarize yourself with the functions available through the menus situated at the top of the screen. You may also find that some additional functions are only available via the submenus of the various floating 'palettes' of an application). The best way to learn the basics and the different functions of individual tools is to set yourself a small, unambitious project. As you gain confidence you will be able to use the program to achieve increasingly complicated commands and effects.

Getting faster

When using a program, remember that there are often many different ways to achieve the same end result and that one solution is not necessarily more valid than another. The main advantage you gain with experience is speed.

When you find that you are using a particular command frequently, train yourself to use the keyboard shortcut (listed in the menu next to the specific command). This is a much more efficient

way of working and will soon become automatic. There are some keyboard shortcuts that are universal across applications, operating at a system level, such as save, open, close, copy, cut, paste and undo.

There are three 'modifier keys' on the keyboard that unlock additional functionality in graphics (and other) software when combined with the mouse, they are: Command (the Apple or Window key), Shift and Option (alt). Usage varies according to the application and the task in which you are engaged, so refer to the manual if you can. In broad terms, Command is used to perform actions such as opening a document (Command O). Option tends to modify a tool or action into using smaller increments, to make specific selections, or to copy-drag an item. Shift generally constrains – for example, to scale objects uniformly or to move them along a fixed axis.

Explore the wider use of your mouse and click, double-click and triple-click on objects, tools and within text to see how this varies your selections. Touch-typing is also a helpful skill to acquire. If you are relatively new to the keyboard, training software or professional courses can be a quick way to learn before you fall into bad habits.

TIP

Learn the phrase 'Select then apply'. When software appears not to do as asked, it is often because you have not correctly selected the area or item that you want the command to apply to.

Health and safety

Repetitive strain injuries are a real danger in a potentially sedentary field such as graphic design, so think carefully about the environment in which you will use the computer. Take time to find a comfortable operating position where you can sit erect at eye level with your screen. The mouse or drawing tablet should be in an easy position for the hand, identical to that of your normal writing posture. Some people find that a pad to elevate the wrist makes it more comfortable to use the mouse. Make sure that your drives and external devices are accessible without the need to bend or stoop.

Sit at least 50cm (20in) away from your screen to protect against eyestrain. Stick a note to your computer or set an alarm to remind you to take a screen-break every half-hour, to stand up, stretch and walk around. Five minutes is about right for a screen break and rather than detracting from the working process, may provide fresh insight into what you are working on. If you are employed, it is your working right to take screen breaks within health and safety legislation, don't be bullied into doing yourself harm.

*Be sure to arrange **your computer workstation** so that you are able to sit comfortably without undue strain on your back. It is worth investing in a fully adjustable office chair that will support you in a healthy posture.*

*A **laptop computer** is a useful item for when you need to work away from your studio. However, you need to be aware that working on a laptop for long periods is not comfortable: most people tend to crouch over the screen because it cannot be placed at eye level.*

Computer hardware

The most basic computer hardware that you require to function as a graphic designer is a computer and screen, keyboard and mouse, a printer and an Internet connection. Add a decent scanner and an external drive to these when you can. Most designers find a fast Internet connection useful and many recommend the use of a graphics tablet. Beyond this configuration you can add all manner of devices, according to the type of work in which you specialize.

*A powerful **Macintosh computer** is an almost compulsory purchase.*

*A **monitor, keyboard and mouse** complete the basic set-up.*

Computer

If you are buying your first computer, consider your budget – the most expensive machine will be at least a third cheaper within a year, and by the time that you absolutely have to upgrade then everything will cost relatively less. For most designers an Apple Macintosh is the computer of choice. Be sure it has plenty of RAM (computer memory) installed so that it is capable of dealing with graphics applications.

Apple are the current hardware market leaders within the design community and some professionals claim that graphics software runs with more speed and stability on these systems. However, a PC with an Windows operating system is perfectly capable of running the standard design industry applications, is arguably more versatile, and usually cheaper. You should read more widely before making your choice and discuss your choice with colleagues and clients to whom you may need to supply files.

Peripherals

Keyboards, mice and graphics tablets

An extended keyboard with up to 15 function keys is desirable; the numeric keypad and page function keys are handy for the designer. Some software shortcuts are unavailable on a more basic keyboard.

An optical mouse is the best choice. This type works by infrared light that detects movement rather than by means of a trackball. Trackball mice may stick occasionally if the ball mechanism becomes clogged with debris. Mice with increased functionality such as two buttons or scrollwheels are favoured by some designers, but are not essential. Laptops use a small square called a trackpad that you trace lightly with your finger. If you find this difficult to use, you can attach a conventional mouse instead. Graphics tablets employ a device that you hold in your hand like a pen, permitting a more fluid and instinctive movement.

Displays

For design work you need a screen that it is at least 17 inches wide (measured horizontally from corner to corner). It needs to be capable of displaying in 'millions of colours' at a high resolution (ask your vendor if you are unsure about this). A modern TFT (flatscreen) display is generally preferred over an old-style CRT (cathode ray tube) screen.

Printers

The cost of a printer that can provide a true colour-matched proof for press is prohibitive for the majority of individual designers or small studios. To check that your layouts work on the printed page, the cheapest inkjet printer will suffice. You will probably need to invest in one that can print on A3 paper. A colour or black-and-white laser printer is a useful addition to your studio for checking colour separations from the page, which an inkjet printer cannot perform sufficently accurately.

Scanners

Scanner technology has advanced greatly in recent years and prices have dropped dramatically. Industrial drum scanners gives the highest quality scan available, but these are beyond the budget of most small-scale design operations. Most flatbed scanners are now good enough to produce press-ready images. Purchase what you feel that you can afford. It is unlikely that you will need a scanner with a bed larger than A4. More demanding scanning jobs can always be sent to a bureau. The best advice is to learn to use your scanner properly; a good scan from an inexpensive machine will far outrank an inept one from the very best model.

Storage

However large your hard disk, you will need some portable storage capacity for both backing up and transferring files. A modern computer has an in-built CD burner, which is ideal for both purposes (you can add an external burner quite cheaply to an older computer). CDs store between 650-800MB of data on relatively durable media. A CD-R (recordable) is a disk that cannot be erased or reused, CD-RW (rewritable) disk is slower to write because the previous information has to be completely erased before rewriting. Both kinds of disk are inexpensive.

*A **printer** is an essential part of your set-up.*

Zip and Jaz drives are popular, reading and writing data faster than CDs on fully rewritable discs that come in a variety of storage capacities. The disks themselves are more expensive than CDs. A more recent alternative to these options is the memory stick, which plugs into the USB slot and allows you to store or transfer files very easily.

The highest capacity storage solution is an additional external hard drive, which is less readily portable but enables you to backup your system and files completely.

Keeping up to date

Computer technology is advancing much faster than almost any other, and much of this hardware advice will date quickly. For example, touch-screen technology for the average consumer is imminent and we can expect DVD to completely supplant CD technology in the not too distant future. Stay informed and research thoroughly before any large purchase.

TIP

Computer and design trade magazines are invaluable for up to-the-minute information on hardware and software innovations, as is the advice of any computer professionals or enthusiasts that you might know personally.

*A **zip drive** is useful for backing up and transferring files*

Software

Choose your applications with care for these are the tools of your trade. Where possible experiment with free downloadable trial versions of software (which will be time-limited or with disabled functionality) before you buy. In making your choices, investigate primarily what suits you best, high-end graphics software is expensive and a bad purchase could leave you stuck with an uncomfortable working practice.

Operating system

The operating system (OS) is the platform from which all your programs work and which provides the set of rules that govern your computer. The two main operating systems that you are likely to encounter are Windows (for PCs) or Macintosh OS (on Apple Macintosh computers). When you initially configure your system it is worth making sure that you have the most recent operating system appropriate to your hardware. Subsequently, be aware that if you upgrade your OS, many of your applications may also require an upgrade (at a cost) in order to continue to function. Software manufacturers also usually unleash major upgrades in an imperfect state, so you are well advised to wait until six months after the initial release date when all the reported bugs have been fixed. Your OS may (with your permission) automatically make safe minor upgrades to itself via the Internet.

Desktop publishing software

DTP software is your primary tool. Industry standards are QuarkXPress™ (Quark Inc.) and InDesign™ (Adobe), which essentially do the same work. Currently, no other DTP application is capable of creating and outputting sophisticated graphic design in the same way. The vast majority of design jobs are processed through one of these programs at some stage. The DTP application is the central hub of a job, creating a single or multi-paged document that is your pasteboard for text, illustration and graphics. DTP packages have some basic graphic creation tools but the most elaborate controls by far are for page layout and typography.

FlightCheck™ (Markzware) is a useful time-saving addition that will check your finished DTP documents for errors and omissions, then collect all of the relevant files and fonts for sending to print.

Microsoft Word (part of Microsoft Office™) is not a useful design tool, but has an important place in your system because Word is so standard in the wider business community. Much of your copy is likely to be supplied in Word format.

*A comprehensive **range of software,** from a photo manipulation program to a page layout application and PDF creation software, is essential.*

Font management

Your operating system will come with a
serviceable collection of licensed fonts. As you
gradually add to these you will find that they
are more easily managed if you install a font
management utility such as Suitcase™ (Extensis)
or Adobe Type Manager™.

PDF software

The PDF (Portable Document Format) created
by Adobe is now the industry standard for
outputting proofs and sending artwork straight to
lithographic plate. Adobe Acrobat™ will convert
files from most graphics applications to PDF
documents, which are then readable on any
machine with the free Acrobat Reader™. The full
version of Acrobat Professional™ contains a full
suite of versatile PDF creation tools.

Graphics applications

Raster-based applications
Rasterized graphics describe an image pixel by
pixel, and are chiefly used for photographs, digital
video, 3-D computer animation, web graphics and
your screen representation (consisting of pixels).
Adobe's Photoshop™ has few, if any, rivals in this
field as a complete tool. Its image manipulation
tools allow you to perform tasks from the subtle
correction of scanned photographs to the creation
of breathtaking multi-layered artworks. Like all
design applications, Photoshop is so complex that
it takes years to fully master.

Painter™ (COREL) is a fascinating raster-based
illustration tool which, though not essential to a
design portfolio, combines well with Photoshop
for complex image effects.

Vector-based graphics applications
Vector graphics are defined mathematically in
terms of points, fills, strokes and effects. It may
be easiest to think of these as images built with
paths. Illustrator™ (Adobe) and Freehand™
(Macromedia) are the most common tools for
working with vectors, although smaller packages
with more limited controls are capable of
producing print-ready graphics of equal quality.

Because vector graphics are fully scalable
without loss of resolution, they are an ideal
format for working innovatively with type, which
can be converted to path shapes without loss.
Illustrator and Freehand are powerful illustration
applications able to produce a visual range
spanning the seemingly hand-drawn to the near
photographic; in combination with PhotoShop
they can craft nearly any image.

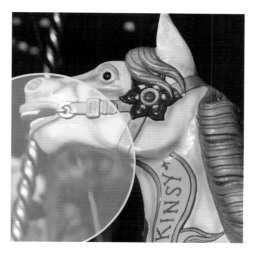

Raster-based images are based on pixels. Photographs
are refined and displayed via a raster-based program
such as Adobe Photoshop™.

*The most common role for **vector applications** is in
originating graphics such as logos or icons. They are also
widely used for creating interesting display type.*

TIP

If you cannot find the exact tools for a specific
design task, then a little web-searching should
yield a vast array of plug-ins ('add on' software)
for your existing applications that might add the
effects and functions that you are looking for.

Manipulating text and pictures on screen

Before you can execute your designs on computer, you will have to assemble and import the elements that you are going to use in your layouts – the text, photographs, and any other illustrative material. Such material often comes from different sources and may be supplied in a variety of formats for which you need to be prepared.

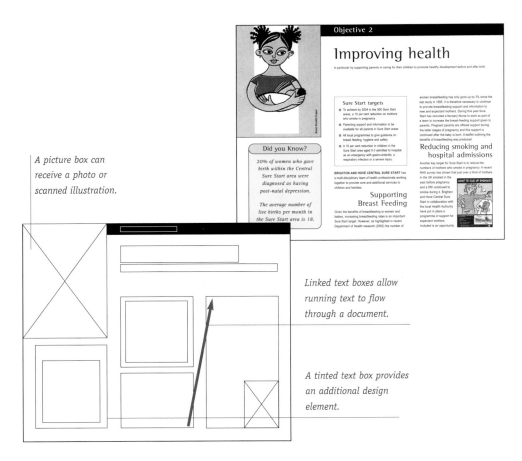

A picture box can receive a photo or scanned illustration.

Linked text boxes allow running text to flow through a document.

A tinted text box provides an additional design element.

Preparing your template

For some projects, for example for a single advertisement, you may be working with live text and pictures as you create your design, playing with the size and position of the elements on the screen. However, for projects that involve many similar pages, such as a book or report, you will need to set up a grid template to provide a consistent structure for the whole job. In QuarkXPress this is usually best created as a Master Page. Using the grid as your guide, you can set up text and picture boxes as necessary, which will then be repeated by default on all the other pages in the document. It is possible to set up a number of Master Pages to cope with variations in design that may be repeated throughout the work.

In a project involving text that runs on from page to page, it is usually most efficient to link the text boxes in a chain. Boxes for separate blocks of text such as captions should not be linked.

Importing text

Text for graphic design projects may be supplied as hard copy, which will need to be typed into the text boxes that you have created in your layout. Usually this only occurs on jobs where the text is minimal, such as a poster. In most cases the client will supply the text digitally, either on CD or as an email attachment. The text is often originated in a specialist word processing program such as Microsoft Word.

To import the text into your layout, you can simply use the 'Get Text' command from the File menu (QuarkXPress), which imports all the text from a selected file into the text box. If you have created linked text boxes the text will flow through the document.

Styling text

In the case of books or magazines the text is usually copy-edited before you receive it, and certain typesetting preferences may have been specified by the editor. However, there will still be plenty of typesetting work to do. In a text-heavy project, it is a good idea to talk to the person preparing the copy so that you can agree conventions for them to communicate any text styling preferences. You may agree to work with a marked-up print out of the text (see page 53) in which text levels and other instructions have been noted. In such cases, you will have to style each block of text individually.

Sometimes the editor may create style sheets in the word processing program. In the case of Microsoft Word, these style sheets can be 'read' by QuarkXPress. To do this the style sheets in Word must have identical names to those you have set up in QuarkXPress. In order to save time and effort, it is well worth taking the trouble to plan this ahead with the client, writer or editor. By using style sheets cleverly you can save yourself some work. But you will nevertheless need to check the text thoroughly for accurate and neat styling (see pages 52–5).

Images in your layout

The technical side of selecting the right image format for output is discussed on pages 98–9. Deciding how to use images on an aesthetic level in your layouts, however, requires a different set of considerations. These relate to the logical placement of images in terms of content and visual balance.

Image selection and placement

In a job where the visuals are paramount, such as an advertisement or poster, picture selection is likely to be largely your decision, subject to the approval of the client. However, in a project where you may be choosing photographs to accompany technical text on a specialist subject, you may find yourself working closely with either an author or editor. It is important for both participants to understand the needs of the other and to co-operate to produce a result that is accurate and useful in terms of content as well as being visually pleasing and harmonious. As a designer you will need to point out when an image is of poor quality or in an unworkable format. But you will also need to respect editorial judgements or the view of experts if you are told that the stunning image you are dying to use is in fact inappropriate for the subject.

When placing images in your layout, you will need to work out what part of the text they relate to and position the illustrations accordingly. In some cases the editor or author may have embedded instructions on picture placement within the text file – look out for this. It may be necessary to make layout adjustments to accommodate the right image – for example, you may need to crop an image to a different format or increase its size.

Designs in progress

Once you have placed both text and images in your design, the files can become quite large and in some cases this can create problems. Some design jobs require several stages of approval and adjustment and it may be inconvenient if your files become too large to send by email to the client for checking. This can be tackled in various ways. A job with many pages can be divided up into several files. Another solution is to use low resolution versions of the image files in your layouts for positional purposes while the design process is in progress, only importing the high resolution files immediately prior to printing.

*This striking photographic image provides the focus of this **brochure cover design**. The dark colours demand reversed out type – a typographic choice that is feasible only where small amounts of relatively large type are needed.*

Image file formats

To fully realize your design concept you need to find the right image. Good designers unable to easily source what they need, will commission or create images themselves. It is equally important to develop a good eye for picture editing and for print, colour and resolution issues. The most breathtaking design will be completely compromised if you use a poor-quality image.

There are a large number of formats in which you can save or receive images. Which format you use or convert to for final output will affect the print quality of the job. Image program document files like Photoshop and Illustrator files should not be used for output to print; you must export a 'flat' version of the file (where the working layers of your image have been compressed) in a print-ready format, remembering to keep your layered working files for future reference.

Resolution

If you look closely at a printed image, with a little magnification you will see that it is composed of tiny overlapping dots. For a designer the size of an image in a layout has two aspects: its physical dimensions (measured in millimetres) and its resolution, which is measured in dpi (dots per inch).

The target resolution for the majority of printed images is 300dpi at 100 per cent of the size of the original. Below this threshold an image will print blurry or pixelated. The resolution of your computer display is 72dpi, so images of this size will look fine on screen even if they cannot be printed. For this reason, 72dpi is the ideal resolution for web graphics.

You can only achieve correct resolution at input stage by making sure that your method of image capture (scan or digital photograph) includes enough image information for your intended printing size. If, for example, you need to enlarge an A5 photograph to A4 (doubling its size), you wil need to scan the image at 100 per cent and at 600dpi. In Photoshop, you can then change the image resolution size to 300dpi with proportions constrained (and without resampling). This will double the physical size of the image but halve its resolution to 300dpi. Similarly, if an image is supplied at 72dpi, you will need to reduce its physical size to about one quarter of the original to achieve a resolution of 300dpi. If you need the image to print larger than this, you must obtain the image at a higher resolution or as a flat image for rescanning.

Be very wary of resampling images. You can resample an image to be smaller without loss of quality, but you cannot increase resolution by resampling – a 72dpi image resampled to 300dpi will look as poor in print as the same image scaled up to 400 per cent.

High-resolution images demand large files. A 300dpi rasterized image uses around 35MB of

*At **300dpi** an image will appear sharp when printed.*

*At **72dpi** the printed image will appear blurry.*

hard disk space. Vector images tend to be smaller depending on their mathematical complexity.

TIFF

TIFF files are stable files for raster graphics. They have the advantage of having excellent screen previews in all DTP applications. A greyscale or bitmap TIFF can also be assigned a colour other than black in your layout program. TIFFs are now supposed to be able to carry embedded clipping paths (preselected areas on the image) but so far, this has proved an imperfect technology.

EPS

This is a format for both raster and vector graphics created using the postscript print information of an image. For this reason they are relatively large files. However, they have the advantage of being able to carry more specific print profile information than TIFFs, such as transparency by embedded clipping path or alpha channel. A vector-based EPS is naturally clipped – only the parts of the image actually described will appear on the printed page. EPS files can preview badly in DTP applications although they may nevertheless print perfectly. Be aware that this is the image file format most likely to corrupt or cause printing problems.

Bitmap

While a greyscale TIFF sees 256 shades of grey, a bitmap (BMP) image shows only black or white. Bitmaps are perfect for images requiring absolute contrast like line art and many logos. Experiment with the creative options to see what suits any given image. Bitmaps require a target output resolution of at least 1200dpi to print accurately but take up little disk space. Bitmap files should be saved as TIFFs.

JPEG

This is the optimum format for web publishing. Cleverly compressed JPEGs produce tiny filesizes that download quickly; however, they should not be used for print. If you need to send a large file to someone then a conversion to JPEG may quarter the filesize for convenience; although bear in mind that the compression (albeit excellent) slightly degrades the JPEG every time it is opened or saved. JPEGs easily paste directly into emails or open in web browsers.

PDFs

Try to avoid using PDF images in layout programs. This is technically messy and potentially problematic. (For more information on PDFs, see pages 110–111.)

Scanning

Final image output is dependent on the quality of the original scan. Professional bureaus and repro houses that use a drum or high-end flatbed scanner make the very best scans. Only an expert who really knows their machine is capable of delivering a foolproof colour-balanced scan, so if a scan is really important then be prepared to pay for it. However, many affordable flat-bed scanners can produce very good results, which can be perfectly adequate for layout purposes or for jobs in which the highest quality is not necessary.

A printed image must be 'descreened' when scanned, or the scanned image will have a patterned effect. A photograph does not require this compensation because it is printed on a grain rather than by overlapping dots. The way to set a scanner for descreening varies between devices, so you will need to read your manual.

Pre-print procedures

Properly preparing a scan for printing is very complex and requires some training and experience. The basic procedure from scan to print is as follows: convert colour mode to LAB, then CMYK, resize to 300dpi, if necessary, adjust levels for colour depth, adjust curves for colour casts and contrasts, clean up dust and scratches before applying a little subtle sharpening as required. The automatic Photoshop filters for cleaning up and sharpening are too clumsy, the former should be done by hand using the clone stamp tool at high magnification, the latter by fine tuning of the Unsharp Mask filter.

*A **desktop scanner** can produce excellent results.*

Web design and the Internet

Design for the Internet requires a more in-depth computing knowledge than for print-based media. The web is maturing as a medium, moving away from its infancy of mimicking the printed page on screen. Websites have become multi-functional; sound, video, animation, games, databases, downloads, purchasing facilities and direct communication are just a few of the many options that can be built into a site. The medium is continuing to expand and we can expect it to evolve into the primary commercial and communication hub during this century.

Web design is fast becoming one of the essential design skills. At the very least, at some stage, you are likely be asked to provide static graphics for the web from your design files. A customer who requires a corporate identity will now probably ask for a simple website to complement their logo and stationery. There is a wider choice of creation tools; industry favourites are Dreamweaver™ (Macromedia), and GoLive™ (Adobe), some still prefer Director™ (Macromedia). However, there are plenty of cheaper and simpler alternatives, for example, a regular QuarkXPress-user might find the interface of Freeway™ (Softpress) friendlier and just as functional at a fraction of the cost. These programs all utilize HTML (Hyper Text Mark-up Language), which is the main programming language for web content. It may therefore be useful to acquire some knowledge of coding to unlock the full abilities of the available software. Some designers are turning to Flash™ (Macromedia) to build all or parts of their sites; Flash is best used as an interactive vector animation tool. It has the advantage of being 'played' by a web browser plug-in, which means that a site can be constructed purely in Flash without using HTML. All web browsers will now play Flash animations as standard.

Image files for the Web

In contrast to print, web design is all about using small, low-resolution graphics that load quickly and look their best on screen. Raster graphics need to be RGB at 72dpi (screen resolution) to the target screen size; usually measured in pixels. Photoshop ImageReady™ (Adobe), which is bundled with the full version of Photoshop, is the perfect tool for exporting files optimized for the Internet. Vector graphics are often preferred because of their small file size. Moreover, the flat colour more usual in vector graphics suits the screen well. You will need to use or convert images to web-safe colours. Your graphics

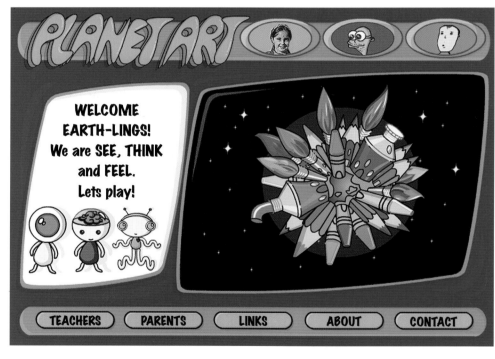

This site for children, teachers and parents was constructed in Flash. A design that would perhaps be garish in print works well on screen. The bold and colourful vector graphics load quickly and animate well. The page is peppered with links to other parts of the site, *the visual cues are obvious and the links 'light up' when the cursor passes over them. From this central 'splash page' we can play a game, read a story, link to related sites, see galleries, email the organization or access a variety of other information.*

applications should have premixed palettes of these. However, if you are unsure, use whole numbers for the RGB percentages. The most suitable file formats for photographs are JPEG (see page 102) and GIF. Aim for as small a file size as possible that still renders well on screen – saving an image without a thumbnail preview will reduce file size and make no practical difference because the target web browser will read it directly. Give your file a short name with the correct file extension (i.e. '.jpg') to avoid cross-compatibility problems between different systems.

Web-page layout

Web pages demand a visual language and structure that is suited to the particular dynamics of using the Internet. There are no chapters, page numbers or indexes in web publications, because everything should be intelligently connected. The way to accustom yourself to the structure of web pages is to simply spend some time surfing the net, research a few things in which you are interested, and see which sites please or frustrate you and why. Poorly made sites will be as revealing in this regard as the excellent ones. Important features to look out for include: clear visual cues such as buttons and links; a logical page sequence and cross-referencing facility; and generally fast, focused and easy operation.

Internet publishing does not have the same technical problems as those associated with print, but it has output problems all of its own, which may need specialist knowledge to avoid or solve. In particular, web pages need to be carefully constructed to work well on all browsers. Once you have constructed a site you may need to pay a small annual subscription for the domain name and will require a server to host the site. Regular maintenance and updating may be required, so if you are offering this service then be sure to factor it into your design fee.

The home page for this image bank serves as a hub for the rest of the site. Here members can log-in and non-members can join or sample a restricted area of the site. The page is peppered with intuitive contextual links to other pages. While some elements appear permanent to visitors, other parts such as the 'new gallery' window (bottom left) may change weekly.

Members home page Having logged into the site, a variety of visual cues allow the visitor to navigate quickly to their area of interest. This site includes a specific search engine to find images that match entered keywords.

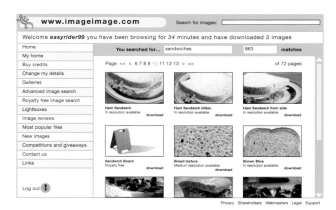

Image browser Searching for an image by keyword brings up results pages of fast-loading thumbnails. Clicking on any one of these will bring up a full-sized image with download information. The visitor can also refine their search, define exactly how to view the thumbnails, add an image to a virtual 'lightbox' for later consideration or navigate to most other parts of the site from this page.

File management and backup

Few of us enjoy housework but neglecting evening chores can leave one with a sink full of washing up in the morning. The consequences of poor computer management are more analogous to waking to find that your entire kitchen has disappeared! You will save yourself hours of time by using a well thought out filing system and can minimize the chance of losing vital data by adhering to rigorous back-up procedures

*An **external CD drive** can provide efficient back-up.*

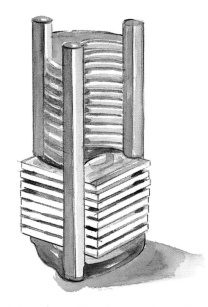

*A **CD storage rack** will help keep your desktop tidy.*

File management

As with paper documents, organization and tidiness in how you handle your computer files will increase your efficiency. Call all your files sensible names – for example, 'Sunflower.tif' is far easier to locate and identify than 'Image 000346'. Always add the appropriate file extension if your software has not done so automatically (for example, for a JPEG file add .jpg). Without such an extension some programs cannot see or open the file. Create a common-sense file structure that makes logical sense to you and reflects your work structures.

One solution could be to make a new folder for each job with subfolders within the main folder in which you group files of the same type, such as images, layouts, supplied copy, illustrator files, and so on. For example, to find the file 'TulipLogo2Colour.eps' the navigation path would be:

Hard disk – Clients – Fantasy Florists – FF Identity – Tulip Logos – TulipLogo2Colour.eps.

Saving

When your computer crashes you will lose all changes made to a document since the last save, so save frequently and habitually. For most of us, saving every five minutes is about right. Use the keyboard shortcut to save quickly without interrupting your workflow. Some applications allow you to set up an autosave option that automatically saves at specified intervals.

Backups and corruption

Computers go wrong. However stable or clean your system, sometimes files just die and will not open ever again. The amount of work that you have lost is defined by when you last made a backup, if you only had one version of a file then everything is gone. Make two versions of any working file and save by overwriting from one to the other occasionally. If a file does corrupt then restart your computer before trying to open your backup, having opened your backup then immediately save a new one.

Bearing in mind the real risk of theft or fire, you should keep copies of all important files on removable media such as CD, Zip disk or tape, and ideally store these in a separate location to that of your computer. You can back up manually but this can be laborious, and you should consider using dedicated backup software that will create copies of all your files on a regular schedule, say at the end of each working day. The wisdom of backing up usually sinks in after you first lose an important job and have to start again from the very beginning.

Software glitches

IT professionals say that a computer cannot go wrong, rather that people instruct it incorrectly by writing 'bad' software. Bear this in mind when you are troubleshooting. If your DTP software keeps crashing, try to remember exactly what you were last doing. It is more likely that an error lies with an image that you were just importing than with the application. Be logical and retrace your steps, restart the machine and try out the same actions in a new document. By finding the exact point of conflict you can usually solve the problem. Be cautious when upgrading any software; make sure that you keep a copy of the old version in case the new one causes problems.

Hygiene

In order to avoid conflicts between extensions and utilities, only add the system extensions that you really need. Be particularly wary of downloading programs from the Internet, unless you are sure that they come from a reputable source. It is essential to install anti-virus software, such as that supplied with Norton Systemworks™ (Symantec), to protect your computer from potentially catastrophic 'infections' often trans-mitted via the Internet or email.

Because of the way that Photoshop and some other graphics applications use your hard disk space to manage their memory requirements, keeping about 20 per cent of your hard-disk capacity free makes the computer speedier with large files and far less likely to crash.

Maintenance and troubleshooting

A busy hard disk needs an occasional service check. This is best achieved using diagnostic and repair software such as Norton Systemworks™ (Symantec) or Techtool™ (Micromat). Running such software once a month is an excellent way of preventing problems. Remember to delete outdated backup files and empty the trash in your email once in a while.

When hardware fails first check and/or replace all leads, connections and plug fuses. Secondly, try the computer on its own without any peripheral devices such as printers or external

drives attached. These are often responsible for apparent hardware failures. Finally, reboot from the system CD to see if the system software is at fault. If so, use repair utilities. If that doesn't work try to get your files copied off the hard disk before you have to reformat it and lose everything.

If a scanner, printer or other external device suddenly fails and you have already checked the connections then uninstall the specific software driver (an option in the original installer software), reboot and reinstall. In the case of an actual physical hardware problem, there is little that you can do other than send it away for repair. A computer is one electrical product where the extended warranty option is a good buy.

Understanding print and film

It is relatively easy to make things look good on screen but translating this to an accurately printed product is another matter entirely. When an error occurs in printing, it is often the result of a mistake by the designer and in an extreme case, you could find yourself responsible for the costs of any reprint. It is therefore vital that you gain a good understanding of the print production process.

In the offset lithography printing process, dots on each colour separated plate overlap when printed to create the illusion of a full range of colours.

Most commercial colour printing uses offset lithography. In this printing process the document is split into individual colour channels representing each of the four printing colours: cyan, magenta, yellow and black (CMYK). The information for each colour is etched on to metal plates. These plates are meticulously aligned so that the miniscule dots that comprise the image overlap but are slightly offset from one another when one colour is printed over another. When viewing the printed image, the eye is tricked into seeing a full range of colours and tints.

Checking separations

The printed plates in our example are called progressives because they are in the actual print colours and are as your printer would see them before combining them to make the whole. The way that design software actually separates for print is by creating a greyscale image for each plate, which are inked in the correct process colours at the printing stage. By learning to look at these separations properly you can check that a job will print correctly before it goes to print. Until recently, separations were run onto acetate prior to the photographic etching of the printing plates. Nowadays it is more common for a job to go 'straight to plate', which is commonly and confusingly referred to as digital printing. In this case, the plates are etched directly without the need for film. The disadvantage is that you no longer have a final opportunity to make a final check for print errors before committing to a print

run. On a straight-to-plate job you must be sure to check paper printouts of your separations carefully and ask for a proof that your printer will commit to.

To check your layouts for printing, you need to output the job from your software as separations rather than a composite image. You can run these to a laser printer for a hard copy or to PDF to check on screen – both processes use actual Postscript print information and are accurate. An inkjet printer is not precise enough for this job. Possible print errors include: fonts unexpectedly emboldening or reflowing, objects not cutting out from a solid background (see Knockout, facing page) and items disappearing entirely. For example, an RGB image that has not been converted to CMYK will not appear on any of the plates of a process colour job – the Red, Green and Blue that your screen uses to define colours are predefined colour channels of their own and would require a separate plate each.

Trapping

Each distinct element of a design is assigned a default trapping setting automatically by your chosen DTP application. This describes how items relate to one another when separated for printing. For example, white text on solid black when separated creates an absence of ink on all plates where the text appears; this is said to 'knockout'. As a rule applications are very good at making trapping judgements and you should only alter these settings if you have detected a print

This full colour image separates into these four plates.   *Yellow*   *Cyan*   *Magenta*   *Black*

problem on your separations or have a specific aim in mind (in which case you will have advanced beyond this advice). Various applications have different methods for dealing with trapping, some allowing control over individual items and some assigning trap styles on a page-by-page basis. The chief trapping settings are:

• **Knockout:** Removes colour from behind the selected element to avoid overprinting.

• **Auto +/Auto:** Behaves like knockout but adds or takes away a tiny increment to an element so that everything fits flush. All inks bleed a tiny bit on paper so this adjustment makes the compensatory visual correction. For example, solid yellow text on a solid cyan background will give the text an auto + trap value, otherwise the bleed from the background will thin the letterforms. Occasionally this trap setting is increased where text runs over two or more other elements of wildly different colour values, making the text appear to be one weight greater half way through (i.e. plain becomes bold).

• **Overprint:** This setting will make your element print over the other items and will therefore darken your target colour if it is printed over

another solid colour. This setting is useful for small text (7pt and below) because it makes registration easier. You cannot overprint white unless you are running white ink as an extra plate.

Laser-printing

For very small print runs it can be more economical to use a colour laser printer. This has the advantage of avoiding most of the technical difficulties described above because it prints a composite image, without requiring separations. However, you need to test the quality first and be careful to perform all the necessary checks if the client later orders a larger offset litho run.

Paper stocks

The final finish of a printed design is also dependent on the type of paper employed. It may be up to you to specify what is used. So if, for example, you want a stiff cover for a report with thinner internal pages then look at your available options for each. Both paper merchants and printers can arrange to have you sent samples of paper stocks from which you can make your choice.

TIP

Sometimes an apparently perfect job will just fail to print, quoting a 'Postscript error' at the separation stage. The error will be attributable to either a corrupt font or bad image. A corrupt font must be replaced, preferably from backup or a new source. A bad image is commonly an EPS file with a clipping path that will need either simply resaving, or in extreme cases the clipping path will require re-originating before resaving.

Setting up a document for print

A successfully printed job is a triumph and the excitement of seeing your first production off the press is not to be underestimated. However, print disasters can cripple both confidence and cash flow. Build as many pre-print checks into the system as you can and do your best to learn from the people who print your work.

Crop marks indicate where the paper will be trimmed. Because paper trimming is not a precise process, any image that is intented to bleed to the edge of the paper needs to extend beyound the crop marks.

Registration marks (above left) are used to check alignment of colour separated layers. Colour markers (above right) help you identify each separation.

Registration

Registration refers to the alignment of the printing plates for the different colours. To facilitate correct registration, registration marks, which appear as 'crosshairs', are printed in a predefined colour within the DTP application on each colour layer. The registration colour is also used to define the crop marks, folds, perforation, cutouts and bleed areas of a document. Many applications can set registration marks for you automatically, which is fine for simple documents. However, for more complex pieces, you will need to set these marks yourself.

Colour information

If you do set your own registration marks, then it helps to put some colour information in the registration area so that there can be no confusion about which plate is which. You can place professional colour bars and some software will do this for you. However, you can simply name each plate in its chosen colour (see left).

Crop marks

Crop marks indicate where a document will be cut to its finished size. They should be set as solid lines 1pt width away from the bleed edge. Fold

marks and perforation marks are traditionally set as dotted lines, where a document uses both and/or is unclear, you may write 'crop' or 'perf' in 7pt registration text next to each relevant mark.

Bleed

The bleed area is a small area of extra image that is outside the intended dimensions of the finished cut product. For safety the bleed area should extend at least 3mm beyond the crop marks. When a job is cut to size, even in the hands of the most skilled operator, the trim is never totally precise. If your design is made exactly to the document edge without an allowance for bleed, you may be left with a thin white line at the edge of the final product, which looks terrible. For the same reason, you should not place any copy that needs to be clearly read less than 3mm from the edge of a document in case it is cut off. When you construct your designs account for this extra little bit of image space off the edge of the document page. At final output stage pull all solid objects out to the bleed area and tell your software to add bleed to the document size for print separations.

Collecting for output

When you have finished and checked a job and are ready to send it to print, you must collect all the relevant files together for output. Always check with the chosen printer or platemaker which file formats they accept. A print-ready PDF can be sent to print as an isolated file providing that the fonts are embedded and the images are uncompressed within the file. A DTP file will also need to be sent with all image files and all typefaces used. When collecting typefaces, include TrueType and Bitmap fonts as single suitcase files, whereas for Postscript fonts, include both the screen and printer fonts, both of which are vital. In addition, you must ensure that the typefaces sent are the versions actually used by your document because a different version might reflow all of your text. The whole process of collecting is gradually becoming simplified by specially designed preflight software that can collect all the files you need for you. Be sure to enclose a hard copy of the job with the files, preferably from a laser printer, so that comparative checks can be made at the printers.

Imposition

Imposition is the term used to describe how the pages of a document are arranged on each side of a printed sheet. Any multi-paged document must work on the basis of a multiple of four because a single folded sheet creates four pages – two on each side. Depending on the size of the pages and the printing sheets there may be up to 32 pages on a single sheet. You should discuss the imposition plan with your printer before finalizing the files. In most cases the printer will provide this for you, so you need only lay out your pages or spreads in the intended sequence.

Cutter guides

For complex print and paper-engineering jobs from folders to cartons, a cutter guide is used. The way that you originate and work with cutter guides is best arrived at through discussion with the person that is printing the job. In the case of most packaging you will work from an existing guide. If a client asks for something unusual it is always worth asking a few printers what templates they have available and seeing whether you can adapt one to your needs as the cheapest and most hassle-free option. Many cutter guides take the form of a vector-based 'wireframe' that fits over the artwork in a separate colour channel and the actual frame that does the finishing is constructed from those measurements. When you make your own cutter guides, the most important thing is that the printer understands what you intend. It is wise to make a proper mock-up from your cutter guide to check that it works correctly and submit this with the artwork files for output.

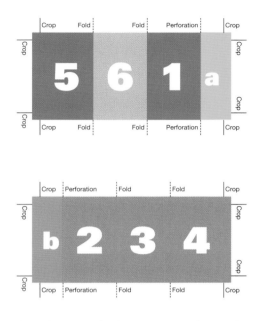

This is the **cutter guide** for a report. A complete set of registration, perforation and fold marks are included.

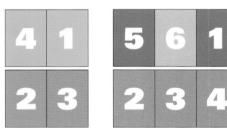

Imposition guides for a simple four-page leaflet and a six-page gate-folded leaflet. Imagine the two sides of each document printed back to back, both folding out to a central spread. The title page is on the 'wrong' right-hand side in layout for print, making perfect sense when folded to form a single cover page. For complex documents such as a large book, the imposition plan is more sophisticated and is best worked out using specialist software.

Process colour

A computer display describes colours in terms of light whereas on the printed page colour is rendered through inks. Never assume that your screen gives an accurate representation of print colours, instead invest in a process colour swatch book or colour reference books (if you can afford it, choose one that also gives you tint values) to check what the printed version of any process colour looks like.

Colour proofing

It is rare for a design budget to allow for the production of a 100 per cent colour-accurate print proof. The most perfect type of proof is called a 'wet proof', which is an early run out from the final press. The presses then wait until the proof is approved before running the rest of the job. Because a large proportion of the cost of printing is in time and labour, the price of a wet proof is prohibitive for all but the largest of print runs. However, the final outputter should offer a reasonably accurate and affordable proofing system. A good current choice is a Sherpa proof, which uses intelligent software and a seven-ink inkjet system. A proof run out of a consumer inkjet or laser printer is less accurate, even with

good calibration and colour-matching software. So it is imperative that you both use printed examples for reference and that you refer your client to actual colour swatches when delivering a proof. Blues, browns, vivid pinks and greens often show the greatest variation in tone and shade between screen, proof and print.

In some cases it can be better to proof entirely electronically by a screen-optimized PDF, partly because it is quick and reasonably colour accurate as a proofing system anyway, and partly because a client will not expect a screen representation to be totally colour matched. Disparities between hard copy proof and final print often seem to surprise more.

*These three **examples of tints**: a 12 per cent yellow and a greyscale image at both 15 per cent and 45 per cent black. The yellow tint prints as a pleasing cream colour but may look far too rich on screen and/or printout. The lighter of the two greyscale tints might be perfect for a subtle background, but the darker shade may deceptively suggest better balance when on screen.*

15 per cent greyscale image

45 per cent greyscale image

12 per cent Yellow

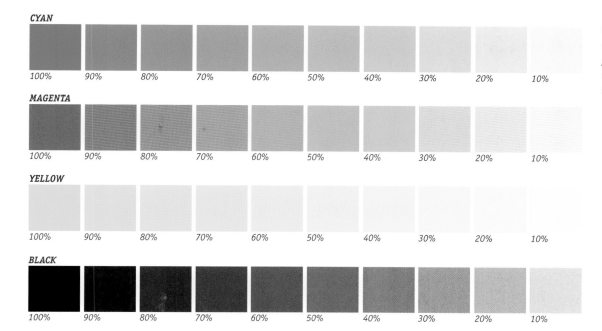

CYAN

| 100% | 90% | 80% | 70% | 60% | 50% | 40% | 30% | 20% | 10% |

MAGENTA

| 100% | 90% | 80% | 70% | 60% | 50% | 40% | 30% | 20% | 10% |

YELLOW

| 100% | 90% | 80% | 70% | 60% | 50% | 40% | 30% | 20% | 10% |

BLACK

| 100% | 90% | 80% | 70% | 60% | 50% | 40% | 30% | 20% | 10% |

Try out the colours in these examples on these pages on your screen and output them on your desktop printer to see the differences between each device and the printed page.

100 per cent cyan overprinted by 100 per cent black – called printers black.

100 per cent magenta, 100 per cent yellow – bright red.

50 per cent magenta, 100 per cent yellow – warm orange.

80 per cent cyan, 100 per cent yellow – emerald green.

100 per cent cyan, 50 per cent magenta – rich blue.

50 per cent cyan, 90 per cent magenta – rich purple.

Some useful colour tints are shown here. You may find it helpful to keep a note of tints that you have used successfully in the past.

TIP

When choosing process colours and tints, you may find that it is easier to convert your desired spot colours to CMYK. However, you must remember that the final CMYK colour will not be exactly the same as the original spot colour and in some cases may differ significantly.

Spot and two-colour work

When money is no object, our design options and the arsenal of inks we can use to achieve them are endless. However, not every client can afford full-colour work, nor does every job require it. In such cases a design that utilizes monochrome or two-colour printing is the best solution.

Monochrome

Single colour or monochrome work is technically the most simple to achieve. It does not, however, have to be seen simply in terms of black and white: the single colour can in fact be any colour and in combination with a coloured paper stock affords many interesting options. For impact and clarity, black or single-colour greyscale images require a little more contrast and sharpness than full-colour equivalents.

Spot colours

A spot colour is a colour other than the standard process colours cyan, magenta, yellow and black (CMYK) that is separated onto printing a plate of its own. There are a vast number of spot colours to choose from, all with slightly different finishes. Popular choices are from the PANTONE™ system and the Coated and FOCOLTONE™ ranges. The commercial makers of spot colours attempt to match their colours across the breadth of the design process from manufacturing and supplying the printing inks, to integrating the colour models into graphics software, to hardware calibration systems. However, the only way to be certain of the printed result is to purchase a swatch book from the manufacturer. A book of tint values is also enormously helpful.

There are many spot colours that simply cannot be duplicated using the CMYK process, but trying to match between the two can be problematic. Bizarrely, a spot colour can be matched to a CMYK colour, which can then be mixed from process colours and singly inked on the plate.

This book uses five colour separations in its production, one each for C, M, Y and K and an additional black separation for all text – commonly termed Text Black. The inks for the two blacks are the same but the fact that the text prints on a separate plate means that it is easy to

*This vector illustration for a surf-wear shop uses just **one spot colour**, the depth of contrast and tone arising from the full range of tint values, compositional balance and variation of line. Although the chosen hue best describes this composition, once made, an image like this will print successfully in any dark colour.*

strip out the text for jobs that are to be printed in more than one language, leaving the images intact and the CMYK plates unchanged.

Some spot colours are loosely grouped under the name 'specials'. These include metallic inks, ultraviolet inks and varnish layers. You can often achieve startling effects with these choices relatively cheaply.

Two-colour work

Two-colour printing is a popular choice for maximum impact on a limited budget. An intelligent approach to this printing option gives scope in complex design that monochrome cannot hope to achieve. It is pointless to opt for three colours (unless one of them is a special) because the cost differential is so slim that one might as well jump to four and therefore full colour.

Selecting two colours

There are many classic colour combinations for two-colour work. It is often wise to choose black as one of your colours, as it is often the best choice for representing both photographic images and text. A very dark colour that gives you some of the qualities of black at 100 per cent solid, but that offers more interest at the other end of the tonal range, is an alternative. Good contrast is desirable in two-colour work so perhaps choose a light colour to counterbalance your dark. If you experiment a little and are clever with your choices then you might be able to squeeze a seemingly third colour out of the combination of your two colours.

Duotones

Rasterized images can be made into duotones using a blend of two spot colours, (the function is found under Mode in the Image menu of Photoshop). Not all images look good in duotone and some colour combinations will never work. A balance of monochrome and duotone images in a document may be effective.

Black and cyan – black image cyan frame

Black and cyan – black image and frame, 8 per cent cyan background

Black and cyan – black and cyan duotone

Purple and orange – purple image orange frame

Purple and orange – purple image and frame, 12 per cent orange background tint

Purple and orange – Purple and orange duotone

Pitfalls

Two-colour work is perhaps more prone to human error than full colour, so checking separations is crucial. When building a design across applications make sure that the same spot colour is used with exactly the same name throughout. It is possible to believe that you have imported the identical colour by reference in different programs and still find that they behave as different spot colours. You can check most easily by looking at the colours in your DTP package because an image will bring its spot-colour information with it into the colour palette when imported.

You must make the halftone screen values of your spot colours different from one another. All spot colours have a default screen angle the same as black (45 degrees). Two or more plates sharing a screen angle will print the dots exactly on top of one another (rather than offset), which will 'muddy' any tonal areas of image and drastically reduce print quality. If you don't know how to make this change using the output configurations of your DTP application then ask the printer to do this for you on output and check before the plates are made that they have done so.

MASTERCLASSES

Drawing for graphics

How an observation or an idea is processed by the brain and then expressed in visual terms is essential to its effective communication. The graphic designer develops a special sense of how problems can be solved and simplified quickly and accurately. This masterclass focuses on a short-hand method of progressing drawing style through both the editing process (paring the information down to the essentials) and appropriate use of graphic mark-makers (to describe the object or concept).

Materials used

Pencils: HB, 2B, selection of coloured pencils

Gouache paints: cobalt blue, French ultramarine, spectrum violet, alizarin crimson, brilliant green, cadmium yellow, cadmium red, cadmium orange, burnt sienna, zinc white.

Brushes: Sable round, no. 2, 6 and 8.

A simple watercolour of a beach scene provided the reference for this task of translating a softer image into a simplified, design-based illustration. The watercolour was unsuitable in its original form because the painterly marks, although very attractive, lacked the clarity required for the task. The graphic designer must make decisions on behalf of the client, where possible keeping the image as simple and communicative as possible. Although this exercise was not for a specific client, it was felt that the original watercolour format was too fussy and required both simplification and a change of media to make it bolder and more vibrant.

1 | **Watercolour study** *This watercolour rendition of sailing near the shore and beach was made rapidly on location one evening in late summer. Its soft, blended qualities, achieved through wet-on-wet technique, although perfect for conveying the sense of mood, place and atmosphere, were not right for a crisper graphic depiction. It was decided that the painting could be used as the basis for a revised, flat, colourful graphic image.*

Techniques used

Tracing
Pencil shading
Washes
Opaque painting (gouache)

2 | **The tracing** *The first step towards simplification was to trace the image onto a sheet of layout paper, secured over the original watercolour with masking tape. After practising on the side of the paper with different grades of pencil, a direct pencil line was delivered with even pressure around the main watercolour shapes. Where necessary, the shapes were filled in with simple vertical line strokes.*

3 | **Adapting the design** *The promenade with beach huts was too complicated and the huts too small to make an impact in this treatment. Most of these elements were removed and the extra space was taken up with trees added with artist's licence. The main focal point of the composition lies in the beached boat and this was further emphasized by enlarging the keel, rigging and sail, with the sail curving towards the right-hand side of the composition. The boats at sea were also simplified into basic, recognizable shapes, and the waves were unified into a rhythmic wave pattern. The shoreline was given strong, controlled curves.*

4 | **Final adjustments** *The main picture was enlarged to fill the sheet. All lines were strengthened to create a strong keyline.*

5 | **First colour rough** *The first colour rough was executed in colour pencil. This presented the idea of solidity and tonal weighting in the picture. Even though the vertical directional shading provided a lively, textured quality, it was decided that a flat-colour effect created with gouache would be more appropriate.*

6 | **Gouache colour rough** *To give a clearer idea of the colour saturation and palette, this rapid gouache rough was produced on cartridge paper using two large round sable brushes (no. 6 and 8). It was not necessary to give care and attention to fine detail, and the colours did not necessarily fill right up to the outlines. This level of execution is usually more than adequate to give a clear indication of the intention of the design to a client.*

7 | **Final artwork stage** *With the correct placement of colour on the rough and all graphic problems solved, time was taken to produce a beautifully finished artwork on a fresh sheet of stretched cartridge paper. A number 2 brush was used to delineate all the straight edges accurately.*

TIP

Thoroughly mix a little white into your gouache paints to prevent them from drying with lumps and streaky colours.

Creating a company logo

Corporate branding is not a new concept. The world of commerce has long relied on brand recognition, so a company's logo must be instantly recognizable and reveal, in a few simple characters and colours, the ethos of the business. The retail sector is especially competitive, with hundreds of thousands of small businesses all vying for their share of the market. This project, to design the new logo for a Mexican takeaway restaurant, follows the graphic designer's thoughts and decisions, from first ideas to completed full-colour artwork.

1 | **The existing logo** *The original logo gave confused messages about the company; it seemed to relate more to sport than Mexican fast food. Note how the 'G' is dominant rather than the word 'chilli'*

Chilli G's, a popular fast food takeaway restaurant, needed a strong, fresh identity that instantly stated the fundamental characteristics of the business. The original logo had been hurriedly designed, and while it had served its purpose on menus, packaging and signage, a change was overdue. In the first meeting with the designer the basics of the brief were decided upon as follows:

• The design should communicate that all food sold is hot.
• It must avoid the stereotypical Mexican images of maracas and sombrero hats.
• The new logo should be clean and legible with a 1950s retro styling to suggest that the company had been around for a long time.

Chilli Gs

Chilli Gs

CHILLI GS

CHILLI GS

Chilli Gs

Chilli Gs

Chilli Gs

Chilli Gs

Chilli Gs

2 | Researching themes *The first stage of research was a visit to the restaurant to sample the food as the best way to gain a feel for the corporate message. The second was to seek out images of Mexico and its foods from the local library. Using simple keyword searches such as 'Mexican' and 'chilli', low-resolution (72 dpi) images were downloaded from various websites for quick initial reference to get some ideas flowing.*

3 | Discarded images *Inevitably there are some avenues of research that prove a dead end. Although strongly suggestive of Mexico, the cactus image did not lend itself to use in the design.*

4 | Researching the font *The designer's initial response was to take a 'blank canvas' and get familiar with the name. By setting it in a variety of fonts, it became clear which of the typefaces wasn't working; some were too plain while others just did not have the right 'feel'. Some traditional fonts were tried out alongside newer, more contemporary faces (from top to bottom): Plantin Bold, Courier New bold, Bertram bold, Brush Script medium, Fontdinerdotcom regular, Fontdinerdotcom Loungey regular, ModularBlack regular, Party plain*

TIP

A logo must be able to work well both small and large over the full range of likely uses, for example, on a business card or an advertising billboard. The design should work equally well in black, two colours, and four colours, again for versatility of usage. Vector-based graphics are most suitable because they can be rescaled and recoloured easily.

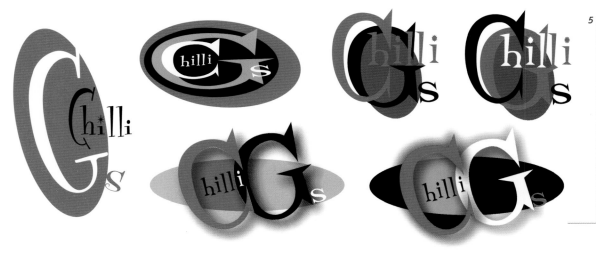

5 **Experimentation** *These early experiments were an attempt to get as much as possible out of colour and type as graphic elements. This is a visual brainstorming of the project; making quick form, juxtaposition and colour choices, pushing and pulling shapes, discarding unsuccessful attempts, while putting anything eye-catching to one side for later assessment. At this stage the free flow of ideas is more important than a high level of finish.*

6 | **Towards a workable idea** *Sometimes the obvious works well: the shape of the chilli-pepper resembled the vertical strokes of the Ls in the word 'chilli'. With an idea forming, followed by a few hours of observational sketching, chilli-peppers were drawn up as new font characters that formed the Ls and the Is. Surprisingly, it was Brush Script, often shunned by designers for its limitations as a font, that proved ideal for the main display typeface.*

7 | **Fine-tuning the type** *To make a specific combination of letterforms work perfectly always requires a bit of tweaking. In this case the G and S needed to be joined. The characters were slightly rotated, edited and combined as vector shapes. Often a typeface will need careful kerning to space evenly as display type, for a logo where a single word or phrase is everything, it pays to be even more fastidious with the letter-spacing. A black 'brush stroke' was applied to the letterforms to add to the hand-drawn feel and to work more harmoniously with the graphic chilli elements.*

8 | **Selecting the colours** *A sheet was prepared demonstrating different colour treatments of the same design. A subtle drop shadow was tried in places to lift the wording from the background and some variety in strap-line and background styles were shown. The greyscale treatments show how any single colour might be made to work. A completely solid colour treatment (bottom row, centre) was shown because some processes such as screenprinting for waterproof food labels cannot reproduce any form of tint or gradient. The initial colour choices were the green, black, red and white of the Mexican flag. While red is visually powerful, and green hints at the freshness of food, as a combination they were simply not 'hot' enough for the product.*

9 | **In the final design** *the predominant colours of red and yellow formed a blistering combination.*

Packaging

We learn to associate certain shapes and colours with certain products and are acutely attuned to the subtleties of their branding. A bright and jazzy design, crammed with information, styled in a number of display typefaces and bold, illustrative images is likely to indicate a mass-market product. An upmarket look is simple, with minimal coloration, often with a single image and simply typeset name and plenty of 'empty' space to set it off.

The brief was to design packaging for a full display range of foodstuffs created for inclusion within a gift hamper for an upmarket foodhall. The brand name Gourmet Foods was to be simply denoted by the letter 'g' set in a friendly, rounded and elegant font for instant recognition. The items for inclusion in the range were a jar of preserves, marmalade, chocolate, shortbread, flapjacks, loose tea, fruit cordial, and a hamper/tray. There was no restriction on the materials or colours that could be used. The design for the range needed to:
• Reflect its natural organic roots effectively.
• Convey a hand-made, quality ethos.
• Provide the customer with all the necessary information about the product.

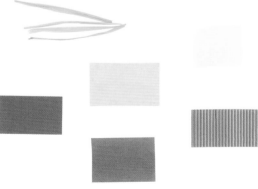

1 | **First thoughts** *Having given careful consideration to all aspects of the brief, ideas were scribbled down on sheets of layout pad and the products for inclusion, including their packet or container, were sketched out in thumbnail form.*

Materials used

Coloured tracing paper
Brown parcel paper
Corrugated card
Thin brown card
Cream card
Raffia
PVA glue
Dry-mount aerosol adhesive
Layout paper
Gold spray paint

2 | **Selecting packaging materials** *Next, suitable materials were selected to suit these organic, upmarket products. The hand-made feel of the merchandise was considered of vital importance in the overall marketing strategy. Textured papers that seemed to meet this requirement were bought from specialist paper shops. Solutions to certain practical problems were also considered at this stage. For example, where textured papers were too thin for use with tags or containers, they were backed onto a thin, brown card.*

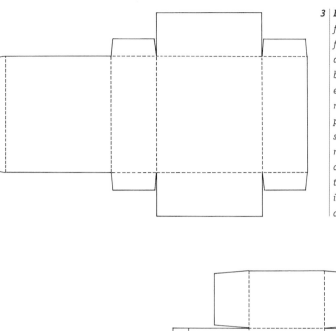

3 | **Designing the nets** *Nets for the chocolate box, flapjack box, tea box, shortbread tube and tray were found in a relevant pattern book and copied. It was decided that for uniformity and continuity of the brand name, all boxes and containers (with the exception of the bottle and preserve pots) would be made from brown card and surfaced with brown parcel paper, according to the individual nets, as shown. For the purposes of short-term display, dry-mount aerosol adhesive was used, because it does not cause any cockling or bubbling of the paper. However, this would not be suitable for long-term display as it is apt to dry out and peel off. Maquettes were constructed in card to test the construction.*

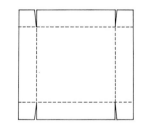

Tools used

Pencil
Scalpel
Scissors
Measuring rule
Safety cutting rule
Cutting mat
Computer (with typesetting program)
Printer

4 | **Designing the labelling** *The materials for the labels were chosen to work with simplicity of colour and typestyle to convey the superior quality of the products. The labels were designed through a number of thumbnail stages. The selected design has a simple 'g' for 'gourmet' set in the elegant font Trebuchet. On the underside of each of the labels is the product type; for example, elderflower cordial and this was set in Blair midi, a copperplate display font. All type was set in black and tonality was created with a covering layer of tracing paper over the type. Where possible the tags and their containers were kept to the square or rectangular format to maintain a sense of unity. The lids of the pots were sprayed gold.*

5 | **The finished boxes** *By this stage, all boxes had been made, as had the selection of pot and jar shapes for the preserve and marmalade. The shortbread tube was constructed with the aid of a larger plastic tubing, around which the cardboard was gently moulded to ease it into shape and prevent unnecessary creasing. The lid was made slightly larger in order to fit snugly. The delicacy of the chocolates required less information on their wrappings – a simple g fixed to corrugated card. The foil wrap and their size and shape gives ample clues as to their identity. This is a classic case of not saying what does not need to be said.*

6 | **The display tray** With all items made, it was time to consider a tray to stand them on. Only at this stage of the project are you in a position to measure out the dimensions of the tray, knowing how much space you will require from setting all the objects together. The idea for the tray was adapted from a container pattern book. Heavy card was surfaced with corrugated cardboard for extra load-bearing strength and robustness. Finely shredded paper was obtained from a specialist paper retailer for lining the tray, adding to the attractiveness of the display.

7 | **The final product** Final presentational extras were now considered. An ingredients list for all the pack products was designed as a concertina fold-out label. The same typefaces set in black were employed as for the other packaging and labelling. All working drawings, thumbnail sketches, maquettes and swatches were filed away safely for future reference.

Poster

Jazz carries the virtuosity of fine musicianship into the exciting territory of improvisation and this needed to be reflected in the poster. In a project of this type, designer and illustrator often team up to work together. Their enthusiastic responses to specific parts of the same brief can produce an inventive hybrid of two creative approaches.

This poster for a jazz festival was the perfect collaborative expression for illustrator and designer. The poster needed to capture the spirit of the festival and reveal certain ideas inherent in the music such as rhythm and connective structure.

A poster should work at a number of levels simultaneously. First, it should convey relevant and concise information and clearly communicate this to the intended audience. There are no hard rules, but a display font is often used at a large size for the main title. Where information is primarily text-based, care must be taken to vary size and style, including perhaps reversing type out of a dark background. Avoid using too many fonts, as these will simply lead to visual confusion and lack of focus. Some of the best posters combine type and image, and sometimes letterforms are used as image. A poster should be eye-catching and colour may well be an important consideration. Creative use of space between text and illustration elements will also allow the design to 'breathe'.

Tools used

Pencil
Watercolour paints
Bockingford watercolour paper, 140gsm
Khadi handmade watercolour paper
Safety cutting rule
Personal computer with layout program, vector-based drawing/graphics program and image-manipulation program.
Printer

1 | **The medium** *Watercolour was the chosen medium because of its freedom and freshness and its ability to produce a wide range of marks on various paper surfaces. The illustrator revelled in the possibilities and produced a series of jazzy expressions for the designer to choose from.*

2 | **Setting the scene** *The coastal venue was deemed important to the event, and a tighter watercolour of the place was created as an anchor point for information. Displaying both hard and soft edged passages of colour with relative simplicity, this fleeting impression of the town painted at dusk with vivid hues of warming blues and diffuse, complementary oranges, helped to set the scene for the event.*

3 | **Type decisions** *A 'clean' and legible typeface was considered the most suitable. The Univers type family was chosen for its broad range of variations from the chunkiness of Univers Black to the stylishly elegant elongation of Univers Light Condensed. Using a page layout program, the word 'jazz' was typed onto a blank A3 document. Along with the paint marks, which had been imported as artwork scans, the type was moved around the page. The freedom of the marks dictated the 'behaviour' of the title to a large extent. Set within typographic rules, the function of the type was as a focus for the design. It was decided to place a tint panel containing the title into the top right-hand corner.*

4 | **Combining elements** *A 303mm x 426mm (A3 plus 3mm bleed all around) CMYK photoshop document was created at 300dpi. All visual elements were scanned slightly larger than needed to allow for flexibility and movement, before being dragged into the photoshop document as floating layers to be scaled, moved and combined.*

5 | **Using tints** *The splashy rhythms of colour that formed the logo were moved creatively within the poster borders, scaling up and down, vignetting, and cropping in the space, to achieve a harmony with the typography and to form those all-important shapes of white space. A white tint panel set to 70 per cent opacity (a 30 per cent tint) was made on the topmost layer for the display type to sit on. Two versions were saved; the flattened artwork as a TIFF file for importing into DTP layout, and the original layered artworking file for easy adjustment if necessary.*

6 | **Finishing touches** *The design lacked something but these watercolour characters would have clashed with the coastal scene in the form provided. The images were first converted to greyscale and a little contrast was applied. The images were then converted to bitmap files using the diffusion dither mode to retain tonal variation.*

7 | **The logo** *The bitmap images were laid over the photoshop TIFF within a DTP application. The double bass player works well with the elongated display type (a stretched Univers Light Condensed), creating an informal logo that could be applied to a range of publicity materials.*

8 | **Incorporating detailed information** *Having created a style in the upper part of the poster, the essential information – venue and date – needed to be included in the lower section of the poster as well as the festival logo. It was vital for this information to be clear, with a logical hierarchy in order of importance. It was also necessary to ensure legibility at a moderate distance and to select font sizes accordingly. All fonts were selected from the Univers family.*

Layout design

Great layout design is about delving deeply into your source material and seeking to understand what needs to be communicated. Armed with this knowledge, you can bring a huge diversity of images and information together in a way that makes sense visually and in terms of content. Implementing a set of structural rules and a precise hierarchy of information provides a framework within which to use your creativity.

The programme whose annual report is shown here, supports pre-school children and parents in a variety of schemes, as well as assisting, supporting and linking related local services. In previous years a strong corporate message had been expressed. On this occasion the annual report needed to refocus towards the needs of parents, volunteers and service users. The first two reports had contained a large amount of statistical and programme data, and the amount and content of the text was largely unappealing to parents. The new information was therefore cut down to the bare essentials and new areas of direct interest were included, such as quotations from service users and tips for childcare. This pared down text was to be used in combination with relevant photography, illustration and children's drawings.

Inital concepts

As the copy was edited and some images were gradually sourced, a design direction began to suggest itself. What if we were to move away from the traditional book type format that we had used before? A height chart for the under-fives on one side seemed like the perfect idea, creating an item of relevance and extended use beyond the report itself. The pages of the report would lie folded within, so in opening up this useful item a parent would be invited to explore the intended

wider meaning. Tips for childcare would take the form of tear-off slips to provide 'free gifts' and increase the relevance and longevity of the document. The designer then began to do some initial paper engineering, and the client looked to source specific images and edit the text to fit this new model.

1 | The Annual Report cover perfectly expresses the core values of the organization with a drawing by a young child. The corporate logo is obvious but unobtrusive. On the bottom of the page an advertising style strap-line invites the service-user to explore the document with a 'FREE HEIGHT CHART', an appropriate gift for the parent of a toddler.

2 | The first annual report had been an economical one-colour document with a full-colour cover. For the second year a more considered two-colour approach was used, designed with a corporate feel and targeted towards the organization's partner services. These text-heavy and weightier formats were succeeded by a smaller and more focused full-colour treatment.

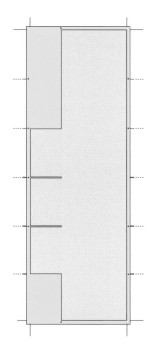

3 | When spread out, the report information occupies one side and the wallchart and front cover make the reverse. The 'upside down' direction of the cover encourages the reader to open the document in the intended way, seeing the report information first and folding out the slips before turning over to discover the height chart.

4 | ***The cutter guide*** *The full document folds five times to make six pages, with the perforated tear-off slips tucking in to make a neat A5 package – careful measuring, the making of a mock-up and consultation with the printer were required to get it absolutely right.*

5 | **Text and typography** *The body copy was broken down into sections. The first and most copy-dense part, which contains lists, finance and reporting, fitted best across the first two pages. Four thematically and stylistically related pages follow beneath, and all five sections were coded in a harmonious colour sequence to divide the content of each part visually. A consistent typographic scheme was applied; the entire body and display copy were set in part of the Ariel typeface family.*

6 | *Pages 3 to 6 (from the top down) share **a common grid** and contain similar data: a main heading, introduction, bulleted list of achievements, two quotations and a pair of images on each page. The grid was transposed further down the page to provide interest and movement.*

I had Hugo on April 17th at the Royal Hospital and he is now a lively gurgling 3½ month old. Throughout my pregnancy, the birth and subsequent home visits, I have felt very well supported and advised by midwives and health visitors.
Zeba Clarke

Sure Start really helped me in those first few confusing, hectic, crazy months after you give birth. I attended the post-natal support group, run by my health visitor, at the Phoenix Community Centre and found it re-assuring and supportive to meet other mums experiencing that mutual roller coaster ride.
I also attended the Park Hill Drop-In on a Thursday (morning) until I returned to work again, which was useful for regular advice, weight checks and meeting other mums. Now I am back at work I really miss it!
Nicky Crabb (Sam Crabb's mum)

Improving Health

Sure Start aims to improve health by supporting parents in caring for their children to promote healthy development before and after birth. During the year:

- **The Sure Start Health Visiting team supported on average over 140 children each month**
- **The Sure Start midwife and health visitors developed and piloted a new model of post-natal extended visiting**
- **The % of women breastfeeding at 6 weeks increased by 6% from 69% to 75%**
- **Sure Start worked with a range of partner agencies to improve the health of families including accident prevention, smoking cessation, healthy eating, emotional well-being and post-natal care**
- **Sure Start established a range of new clinics and groups during the year including a Positive Parenting Group; a post-natal clinic; a joint Health Visiting / Playlink drop-in**
- **The % of pregnant women smoking during pregnancy fell by 3% from 23% to 20%.**

7 | **Quotations** *sit outside and away from the body copy in a box bounded by large Zapf Dingbats quotation marks. Images appropriate to the text were introduced here. The main heading and introduction sit on the background tint over the bulleted achievement list within a stronger box. The tonal values and type sizes of each element separate the immediate information from the more introspective.*

8 | **Combining images and words** *Images came in the form of photographs of groups and service users, whose permission had been sought, and a large bundle of lovely children's drawings. It had been decided from initial sketches that a nautical theme would suit the height chart, so a member of the programme staff with excellent painting skills was persuaded to create some illustrations working to this brief.*

9 | **The wallchart** *For the wallchart, the original illustrations were scanned to size and some extra colour and contrast added before careful clipping paths were applied. The whole image could have been achieved using a vector-based program. However, because the source material was raster based and the rest of the document was set up in a complex QuarkXPress document, the whole image was built in the DTP application using the clipped images. Creating this image was a much more freeform process than for the formal pages. The chief design considerations were where the page folds would lie, along with the clarity and accuracy of the measurement information.*

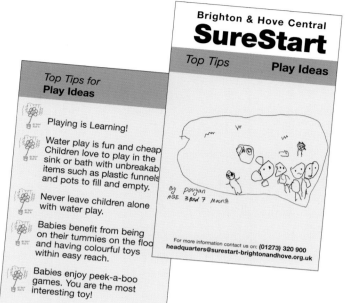

10 | **Tear-off slips** *The tear off slips loosely relate to the section pages that they face in the report, with an appropriate child's drawing on the reverse. Their upside-down aspect on the chart side of the document was intended to encourage the reader to remove and use them, thus extending the function of the original information document. Delivery of information, multiple purpose, targeted advertising, brand awareness and a sense of play all communicate cleanly in a neat and enjoyable package*

TIP

Brilliant design doesn't have to cost the earth. Pool your resources by both playing to your own skills and fully investigating what talents and services your client can call on when creating your designs.

Glossary

Acetate

Clear plastic film used as an overlay on visuals to show separate layers, or used for colour separations on actual artwork.

Alignment

The arrangement of letters or words on the same horizontal or vertical line.

Application

Computer software that serves a particular function, for example, page layout.

Ascender

The part of a lower-case letter that rises above the body (x-height) of the type.

Back-up

(1) Printing on other side of a sheet of paper. (2) Computer terminology: the copying of important work onto portable hard drives, floppy disks, CDs or other external storage systems.

Baseline

The line on a computer grid or layout on which the base of upper-case letters sit.

Bit

A contraction of 'binary digit', a bit is the smallest unit of information used by a computer.

Bitmap

An image or typeform made from a pattern of dots called pixels to be viewed on screen or printed out.

Bleed

Part of an image extending beyond the 'trim' or cut-marks of the page.

Body copy (type)

The bulk of the text of a publication. Body copy is usually set in type of less than 14 point.

Browser

Computer program allowing you to view and interact with Internet pages.

Bubblejet printer

A type of inkjet printer that relies on a heated element to create bubbles which in turn eject ink.

Byte

A unit of computer information consisting of eight bits.

Camera-ready copy/artwork

Finished layout of text and/or images ready for scanning or photographic reproduction. Also called 'mechanicals'.

Cap-height

The height of an upper-case (capital) letter that has neither ascenders nor descenders.

CD-Rom

An abbreviation of compact disc read-only memory. A plastic disc onto which information is written by laser beam. The storage capacity for a standard CD is 650MB.

Clip art

Copyright-free images.

Clipping path

A computer term for the line created by cutting out all or part of an image in a page layout or image manipulation program.

Collagraph

An artist's printmaking technique that involves printing directly from textured materials fixed to a plate to create a raised surface.

Complementary colour

One of a pair of colours that sit opposite one another on the colour wheel. The complementary of a primary colour is a combination of the two remaining primaries.

Composition

The arrangement in a design of visual elements such as colour, light and shade, shapes, lines and stresses.

Concertina fold

Also known as accordion fold, in which two or more parallel folds are made in opposing directions.

Copy

Matter to be set for printing, usually referring to text.

Copyright

The right in law to prevent the copying of written work, images or designs.

Cut-out

Illustration or photograph where certain background sections have been removed to make the subject stand out. Also the physical removal of a shape or defined object from its background of card or paper with scissors or a craft knife.

Descender

The part of a lower-case letter that extends below the baseline.

Display type

Larger (usually 14 point or above) typefaces designed for headings.

Document

In a computer context, any file containing layouts, text or artwork.

DPI

Dots per inch, the measurement that defines the resolution of an image. The greater number of dots per inch, the sharper the image.

DPS

An abbreviation for double-page spread. Left- and right-hand pages designed as a single unit.

Drop cap

A large capital letter that descends below the baseline, usually used as a device to signal the beginning of a section of text. It has its origins in the decorative letterforms drawn by the medieval manuscript writers.

DTP

Desktop publishing. The term includes all forms of computerized page make-up.

Dummy

The prototype of a page-based product, such as a leaflet or book.

Duotone

A halftone illustration or photograph based on the full tonal range, printed in two colours.

Em

A unit of linear measurement used in typography equal to the width of a capital M in the typesize in use. A 12-point (4.2mm) em is known as a pica.

E-mail

Electronic mail. An electronic text message sent through a modem down the telephone line to another user via an Internet service provider.

Embossing

A paper manipulation and finishing technique involving stamping or shaping under pressure to produce low-relief images or type on the paper surface.

En

Half an em, the width of a capital N.

EPS

Encapsulated postscript. A computer format for transferring linear and tonal information into digital layout programs.

Etching

Printmaking process using acid to bite into a plate where drawn or surface marks have not been stopped out with a protective ground.

Family

In typography, a set of fonts with common design characteristics, but of different weights and styles – for example, roman, italic and bold.

Flatplan

A diagram showing the position of pages in a publication with a brief description of content.

Folding

The folding of a flat sheet into book pages. Always a multiple of four.

Folio

The page number printed on a page. Also a term for a single sheet of a manuscript.

Font

A complete set of alphabet characters, upper- and lower-case and their associated punctuation marks, numerals, signs and symbols.

Foot

The bottom margin of a page.

GIF

Graphic Interchange Format. Computer format for graphic images containing flat areas of colour.

Gouache

Opaque, water-based paint that dries in a flat, matt colour.

Grid

The structure for a page layout, printed onto layout paper, or set up in a document within a computer layout program.

Gutter

The margins on either side of the spine where a book or other publication normally folds. It also refers to the space between columns.

Half title

The title of a book as printed on the page preceding the title page.

Halftone

An image of continuous tonal values created by a pattern of dots also of varying tonal weights.

Hard copy

A paper proof of computer-based document or information.

Hard disk

The chief permanent storage unit of a computer.

Hardware

The physical parts of the computer and peripheral devices.

Home page

The main page of an Internet site from which other links may stem.

House style

The consistent treatment of typestyle, punctuation, spelling, spacing and general layout used by a publishing house.

Hue

Another name for a spectral colour such as red or blue.

Icon

A small graphic image seen on the computer screen that represents an application, tool or document.

Imposition

The arrangement of pages in preparation for printing, so that after printing, folding and trimming, all pages appear in the correct page order and are the correct way up.

Indentation
A setting short of the column measure.

Inkjet printing.
A method of printing in which fine nozzle jets accurately spray tiny drops of ink onto the paper.

JPEG
Joint photographic experts group. A format suitable for supporting continuous, tonal colour images, such as photographs.

Justified
Type set to align to both left and right margins. Spacing may vary between words on different lines with justified type.

Keyline
The marks on overlays that enable various layers to be positioned correctly for print.

Kerning
Adjustment to the space between individual letters. Closing or opening the gap can assist the aesthetics of a design.

Leading
The space between lines of type.

Line artwork
Artwork in black and white containing no tonal variation and therefore no dot pattern screen.

Linocut
A relief technique of printmaking, where linoleum is cut away to create negative space, and the remaining material inked up and printed in a solid colour as a positive.

Lithography
A method of printing from a dampened, flat surface using greasy inks. The technique is based on the fact that grease repels water.

Lower-case
Small letter type, not capital letters or upper-case.

Margins
The blank areas surrounding a page.

Mask
A shape cut out of opaque material to shield a film from exposure to light. Also in computer terms, a layer protecting a lower layer from certain digital treatments.

Measure
The width of a line of type, normally the column width measured in picas or ems.

Menu
A list of commands or computer options.

Modem
A device that transfers digital data from computer to telephone line and vice versa.

Mouse
Small hand-held device used to move the cursor on the computer screen and to select options from on-screen menus.

Opaque
Non-transparent medium through which light cannot pass. Also, non transparency in printing papers.

Orphan
Single word or a few words that form a line of its/their own at the end of a paragraph. Usually less than a third of a measure.

Out of register
Blurring on a printed page caused by poorly aligned separations.

Overlay
A sheet of acetate or tracing paper containing flat colour or keyline information, or notes for the printer.

Overprint
Colour printed over another flat colour, often black.

Page proof
A print-out showing all elements in position, including folios, headings, text and illustrations.

Pagination
The sequence of pages in a publication.

Paste-up
Cutting and assembling graphic elements and text/type onto a board with wax or glue. Computer term (paste) moving and duplicating elements into a document, often after copying from another document (copy, cut and paste).

PDF
Portable document format. A format that displays fonts and digital images in a page layout.

PC
Personal computer. An independent desktop computer. The term PC is often used specifically for IBM-compatible computers – that is, non-Macintosh machines.

Pica
A type measurement the width of a 12-point M or $\frac{1}{6}$ inch.

Pixel
The dot on a computer display. Resolution (image quality) is measured by the number of horizontal dots against the number of vertical scan lines.

Point
The smallest type measure equal to $\frac{1}{72}$ inch. Twelve points make a pica.

Proof
Hard copy of a page for checking type, position of design elements, and colour quality, before printing. Proofs can be created at various stages, depending on

the aspect to be checked, including laser prints from DTP files and various types of printer's proof.

RAM
Random access memory. Memory embedded in a microchip in the computer enabling quick access of current data and working programs.

Ranged left/right
Alignment of type to a vertical axis from the right or left, with the text on the non-ranged side appearing 'ragged'.

Raster
Horizontal scan line on a computer screen.

Recto
The right-hand page.

Registration
Correct positioning of colour separations in relation to each other for printing. Registration marks assist this alignment.

Relief printing
Where ink lies on a raised surface and not in the rebated area. The raised surface is inked up and printed under pressure.

Resolution
The measure of fineness or sharpness of a digital image, usually expressed in dots per inch (DPI).

Retouching
Modifying an image either by hand with airbrush and brushes or in a computer image-manipulation program.

Reversed out
White type on a dark-coloured or black panel.

Rivers
Distracting patterns that flow through text created by linked spaces between words, usually in justified text.

Roman
Normal, upright type that is not bold, italic, light, black, etc.

Runaround
Type set around a design element such as a picture.

Running heads
Headings that appear on each page and in the same place, usually at the top. Running heads may differ on left- and right-hand pages and consist, for example, of the book title on one side and the chapter heading on the other.

Sans serif
A typeface without serifs.

Scaling
Reducing or enlarging, normally referring to an image.

Scanner
A piece of equipment used to convert an image such as a photograph into digital information.

Scoring
Creasing a sheet of paper or card to allow it to fold cleanly and easily.

Screen-printing
A printing process that uses a stencil and fine mesh screen. Ink is forced through the mesh, which prints only through the cut-out parts of the stencil.

Serif
The small flourishing strokes at the end of the main strokes of a letterform.

Software
Programs, applications or a list of instructions that enable a computer to carry out specific functions.

Spot colour
Single printed colour printed in register with black.

Thumbnail
Small sketch or first design idea to be developed.

TIFF
Tagged image file format. A file format commonly used for digital scanned images for use in page layout programs.

Tracking
Adjustment to the spacing between all letters.

Typeface
A designed letter with distinctive styling and characteristics.

Upper-case
Large letters, also known as capitals.

Verso
Left-hand page.

Vignette
A half-tone image that fades into the surrounding page area.

Widow
A single word or part of a word from the end of a paragraph that is isolated at the top of a new column or page.

X-height
The height, excluding ascenders and descenders, of a lower-case letter in a particular typeface.

Index

Authors' Acknowledgements

This book is dedicated to those students past, present and future, whose enthusiasm for the craft makes it all worthwhile.

Thanks to Anna Cheifetz and the team at Cassell Illustrated for accepting this title into the series, Katie Cowan at Essential Works for toiling so hard to guide its progress into completion, and Kate, Cathy and Kathy for such excellent editorial and design work.

Thanks too to the members of staff and the students at The Kent Institute Of Art And Design in Rochester, and those at Northbrook College, Worthing, for supporting us in all our endeavours. Special thanks to Colin Jackson at KIAD, for his photographic skills.

Curtis Tappenden wishes to thank his much admired colleagues and friends, Stella Farris and Luke Jefford for enthusiastically backing this book idea from its inception and for agreeing to lend their expertise, insight and skills as co-authors, designers and educators. Without their invaluable contribution this book could not have existed. To his wife Susanne and children, Tilly and Noah – love and gratitude. To Pete at Café Motu for providing the coffee. Final thanks to illustrator, Alan Baker, photographers, Gill Orsman and Nina Chubb-Webster, and newspaper graphic artist, Martin Northrop, for truly professional examples, and to student Daniel Lay for exciting coursework contributions.

Luke Jefford thanks Mike Skinner for his understanding, his wife Kate for her continued love and support and daughters Iris and Ruby for making it all worthwhile.

Stella Farris would like to thank Curtis for the opportunity to collaborate on this book and also for his never-ending support and text messages and Seth Kay for his help with the artwork

Picture Credits & Permissions

Stella Farris 48–9, 48–49, 80–91, 126–129; Luke Jefford and Curtis Tappenden 92–93, 116–117, 130–133; Luke Jefford p. 58, p. 65 (tr), p. 75 (b), p. 99, pp.100-101, 105, 108, 109, 110, 111, 112, 113, 114, 122–125, 134–137 (Photographs appearing in the design work of Luke Jefford on pp 75, 99, 101, 105, 109, 110, 112, 115 and 123 are kindly supplied by istockphoto (www.istockphoto.com); Curtis Tappenden pp. 1–4, pp14-33 pp. 38–43. p. 61, p. 64, pp 67–68, pp 72–73, pp 95–98, p. 103, pp. 106–107, pp. 118–121

Alan Baker (www.alanbakeronline.com) p. 65 (tl): Chris Burton p.57 (r) ; Cassell Illustrated – p. 61 (b) 10 Minute Yoga (Cassell & Co 2001), p.62 Just One Pot (Cassell Illustrated 2004), p.74 Just Like Mother (Cassell Illustrated 2003), p.76 Hippie (Octopus France 2003); Corbis p. 69–71, pp. 102; Nina Chubb-Webster p. 60; Essential Works p. 11, p. 59p. 75 (t); Daniel Lay pp.34–37; Martin Northrop p. 66; Gill Orsman (www.gillorsman.com) p. 63; Matt Pagett for QU:ID; Nick Plackett pp. 57 (r and m) and p. 61;Yuki Sawada (www.loopydog.co.uk for Jellyvision) p. 104; Topfoto pp. 7, 8 (Arena PAL) and 10 (The Image Works): Justin Watson p. 57 (l).

The following typefaces have been kindly supplied by Linotype Library GmbH and are available at www.linotype.com.: Hevetica Neue, ITC Quay, Sans, Modern, Officina, Bauer Bodoni, Dorchester Script, Gill Sans 1, Goudy Text, Minion, Plantin, Shelly

Essential Works

Project Editor	Cathy Meuss
Designers	Kathy Gammon and Kate Ward
Proof Reader	Karen Fitzpatrick
Indexer	Dorothy Frame
Packaging Photography	Colin Jackson